THE SICK TRANS PERSON
Negotiations, Healthcare, and the Tension of Demedicalization

Evelyn Callahan

P

First published in Great Britain in 2026 by

Policy Press, an imprint of
Bristol University Press
University of Bristol
1–9 Old Park Hill
Bristol
BS2 8BB
UK
t: +44 (0)117 374 6645
e: bup-info@bristol.ac.uk

Details of international sales and distribution partners are available at
policy.bristoluniversitypress.co.uk

© Bristol University Press 2026

British Library Cataloguing in Publication Data
A catalogue record for this book is available from the British Library

ISBN 978-1-4473-7110-6 hardcover
ISBN 978-1-4473-7111-3 paperback
ISBN 978-1-4473-7112-0 ePub
ISBN 978-1-4473-7113-7 ePdf

The right of Evelyn Callahan to be identified as author of this work has been asserted by them in accordance with the Copyright, Designs and Patents Act 1988.

All rights reserved: no part of this publication may be reproduced, stored in a retrieval system, or transmitted in any form or by any means, electronic, mechanical, photocopying, recording, or otherwise without the prior permission of Bristol University Press.

Every reasonable effort has been made to obtain permission to reproduce copyrighted material. If, however, anyone knows of an oversight, please contact the publisher.

The statements and opinions contained within this publication are solely those of the author and not of the University of Bristol or Bristol University Press. The University of Bristol and Bristol University Press disclaim responsibility for any injury to persons or property resulting from any material published in this publication.

Bristol University Press and Policy Press work to counter discrimination on
grounds of gender, race, disability, age and sexuality.

Cover design: Robin Hawes
Front cover image: iStock/rambo182

Bristol University Press' authorised representative in the European Union is:
Easy Access System Europe, Mustamäe tee 50, 10621 Tallinn, Estonia,
Email: gpsr.requests@easproject.com

This book is dedicated to all the trans people who came before me and made my existence more possible, and for all those who will come after me that I may do the same.

Contents

Acknowledgments		vi
Introduction		1
1	Trans methodology	15
2	Models of sex and gender	26
3	Re-understanding sex and gender	37
4	Medicalization	55
5	Bureaucracy, time, and space	77
6	Pedagogy and TransLiteracy	102
Conclusion		124
Notes		129
References		135
Index		146

Acknowledgments

Firstly I need to thank my PhD supervisor, Dr. Meredith Jones, for her unwavering support and expert guidance. I must also thank my secondary supervisor Dr. Isak Niehaus and my research development advisor Dr. Hauke Riesch for their help at every stage of my PhD, as well as Dr. Sara De Benedictis and Dr. Grant Peterson for serving on my review panels and offering invaluable feedback throughout the early writing process. And to my undergraduate supervisor Dr. Pamela Erickson, thank you for sparking my passion for this work all those years ago in your medical anthropology class and making this path seem possible.

Huge thanks as well to all of the trans people who took part in this project. I am in awe of the generosity you showed me with your time and your stories. Special thanks to Persé De Ascensao-Pineau for acting as a sensitivity reader. I also owe so much to the broader trans communities for their support and fellowship and to J.T., the first person I ever saw myself in, for showing me that I could live authentically and thrive.

Additionally, I need to thank my family for their unconditional love and support. Particular thanks to my sister Christine, who let me drone on endlessly about my work. It was during a phone call with her where I was explaining what each chapter was about that I realized what the structure of this book should be. And to my mom, thank you for always supporting this dream even when it took me far from home. To my Pink Singers family, thank you for bringing endless joy into my life, I would never have gotten through this without you all. Finally, I need to thank my most patient sounding board, my kindest editor, and my loudest cheerleader, my husband Will.

Introduction

This book analyzes trans health in the UK through two key questions. Firstly, what barriers are there between trans people and the ability to access quality healthcare? Secondly, when they are able to at all, how do trans people overcome those barriers? I have found that there are significant and unique obstacles that delay or prevent trans people from accessing both transition and non-transition related healthcare. However, I have also found that in many cases trans people are able to overcome or at least push back against these barriers in creative and effective ways. Understanding these barriers suggests demedicalization as a solution, which brings up a central tension that will be addressed in this book, one between demedicalizing transness and ensuring continued access to medical technologies for trans people who require them. Additionally, I outline a trans methodology which has developed throughout the course of this research. Overall this work paints a picture of a healthcare system struggling to meet the needs of a population and illuminates what we can learn from that population's response to that struggle.

Disciplinary home

Throughout this book I draw inspiration and knowledge from multiple disciplines, but ultimately the best home for this work is trans studies. While fairly new, the field of trans studies has a growing body of work and is interdisciplinary and deeply socially engaged in nature. In '(De)Subjugated Knowledges: An Introduction to Transgender Studies', Susan Stryker describes the field thusly:

> Most broadly conceived, the field of transgender is concerned with anything that disrupts, denaturalizes, rearticulates, and makes visible the normative linkages we generally assume to exist between the biological specificity of the sexually differentiated human body, the social roles and statuses that a particular form of body is expected to occupy, the subjectively experienced relationship between a gendered sense of self and social expectations of gender-role performance, and the cultural mechanisms that work to sustain or thwart specific configurations of gendered personhood. (Stryker, 2006: 3)

This description not only fits this book but is a road map for the kind of questions I hope to continue to explore throughout my career.
My previous academic background is in anthropology, specifically medical anthropology, and I draw on that background heavily in the development of

this work, particularly in terms of understanding medical systems as part of culture. With this project however I leaned more toward sociological theories to understand gender as a social position and the ways that transphobia and cisnormativity operate in society. The subtle mix of medical anthropology and sociology are prevalent throughout but I also draw on feminist studies, queer studies, psychology, philosophy, biology, and medicine. Using this kind of interdisciplinary approach to better understand trans experiences along with the methodology that I will outline later situates this work within the now well established discipline of trans studies.

Importance

The importance of this research on a more basic level is to help illuminate barriers that trans people face when accessing healthcare. Identifying these barriers is the first step to having them removed and the often creative solutions trans people find to get around or at least push back against these barriers may inspire broader solutions including policy change. In a much larger sense this work says something about the human condition. All people have a relationship to gender, it is simply the case that with trans people that relationship is brought to the fore, making it an excellent vessel for discussing how gender operates. This work oscillates between the small, specific, and personal details that make up lived experiences, and discussions of a fundamentally changing paradigm of what it means to be human through a (re)understanding of gender.

Personal importance

In addition to the reasons stated earlier, this topic is of personal importance to me as a trans person living in the U.K. With a background in critical medical anthropology, I always seek the 'real world' application of my research and focus my academic work on pursuits that will be of service to the communities I work with. Having completed previous research projects that I felt were of service (but to communities to which I do not belong) coupled with my increasing involvement in trans communities[1] following a growing understanding of my own relationship with gender, I embarked on this project. I felt almost an obligation to use this opportunity, perhaps selfishly, to develop knowledge that will hopefully help improve access to and quality of healthcare for myself and other 'gender outlaws', to borrow Kate Bornstein's term, like me.

Research

The research base for this book consists of ten interviews with nine participants conducted in London in the mid to late 2010s. These interviews were recorded, transcribed, and analyzed using thematic analysis.

Participants

Throughout the book I will be referring to all of the participants by the first name I chose for them, but I would like to give a more detailed introduction to them all here. I am recounting their race, gender, and pronouns verbatim in the ways they were explained to me in the interviews. All ages given here are the age they were at the time I interviewed them. For myself I have given my age at the time of writing this book.

- Adam is a 34-year-old white man who uses he/him/his pronouns.
- Ben is a 24-year-old Arab transmasculine person who uses he pronouns.
- Carey is a 21-year-old white British non-binary/agender person who uses they/them pronouns.
- Dan is a 34-year-old mixed race man who uses he pronouns.
- Emily is a 69-year-old white British trans female who uses she pronouns.
- Flora is a 20-year-old white British person who described their gender as "non-binary, gender fluid, transmasculine but I also feel like I'm really femme ... just yeah an affinity with all of those" and uses they/them pronouns.
- George is a 28-year-old white Welsh male who uses him pronouns.
- Holly is a 40-year-old mixed (white and middle-eastern) non-binary person who uses she pronouns and explained "I don't feel the need to identify specifically in the non-binary umbrella, I would feel more on the female side of the spectrum but not necessarily one".
- Ingrid is a 60-year-old white Welsh female who uses she/her pronouns.
- I am a 30-year-old white non-binary, transmasculine person who uses they/them pronouns.

In order to keep the participants anonymous I have chosen pseudonyms for them and generalized or left out potentially identifying details. I chose pseudonyms by letter of the alphabet, so the first participant has an A name, the second a B name, and so on. Beyond the first letter however I did put thought into the names I chose. I tried to choose names with a similar gendered connotation to the name the participant went by. Adam, for example, has a typically masculine name so I chose a typically masculine pseudonym for him. Carey has a traditionally gender-neutral name so I chose a similarly gender-neutral name for them. I did this not because there is anything inherently gendered about names. Indeed, the same name can be gendered differently cross-culturally, for example Hillary in the UK versus the US. I certainly am not invested in naturalizing the gendered connotations of names, however, I cannot ignore the fact that names do have such connotations and that the participants chose their names with the knowledge of how those names are read in the social spheres they occupy.

The participant I have called Flora is transmasculine and has changed their name, but they kept a typically feminine first name (but have a typically masculine middle name). To select a traditionally gender-neutral or masculine name for them because of their gender would erase that very conscious and interesting choice that they made. Additionally, all of the participants also had fairly common English names so the chosen names reflect that as well.

Overview of chapters

Trans methodology

In Chapter 1 I describe the methodology that has developed throughout this research. I begin by laying out my formulation of an ethics of a specifically trans methodology. Following trans scholars Paul B. Preciado, Lucas Crawford, and others, and inspired by other minority studies, I describe the highly community focused approach to research, analysis, and dissemination that I took while completing this work, as well as ways that I can move toward an even more community centered approach with future research. I conclude by explaining how I use autoethnography in this work, following many trans scholars including Dean Spade and J.R. Latham.

Models of sex and gender

In Chapter 2 I analyze existing models for sex, gender, and the relationship between those concepts. To do this I look at the work of Emily Martin and Anne Fausto-Sterling to lay out how our understanding of 'biological sex' is influenced by cultural ideas of gender. This leads to the problematic idea that there are 'male' and 'female' bodies and that the only possible explanation for trans existence is that trans people were 'born in the wrong body' (Bettcher, 2014). I unpack the problems associated with this model, and critically address some alternative models including the 'beyond the binary' model.

Re-understanding sex and gender

I then explore, in Chapter 3, how sex and gender are actually attributed (Kessler and McKenna, 1978/2006; Blackless et al, 2000; Roughgarden, 2004/2013). I try, and fail, to concretely define male-bodiedness and female-bodiedness and so instead explore how sexes and genders are assigned, both in everyday life and in healthcare settings. I then challenge the need for attributing sex and gender to others in the first place and propose a model of sex and gender where these concepts are equally socially constructed and can only be determined and articulated by the individual. I conclude by arguing for moving past an understanding of sex and gender as completely separate and unrelated phenomena and toward one that comes to terms with the ways in which they are intertwined.

Medicalization

In Chapter 4 I argue for the demedicalization of transness as a key way to remove existing barriers to health. The National Health Service (NHS) uses a diagnosis of 'gender dysphoria' which can also be referred to as 'gender identity disorder'. This diagnosis and the corresponding 'treatments' of psychotherapy, hormone replacement therapy (HRT), and assorted surgeries represent the contemporary medicalized model of transness in the UK. To best understand how medicalization operates and therefore how to counter it I use the extensive work of Peter Conrad, outlining the classificatory system which distinguishes between conceptual, institutional, and interactional medicalization, all of which can be understood as functioning toward the medicalization of transness. Conrad also differentiates between deviant and natural life course medicalized behavior. However, in this instance, I depart from Conrad and propose that transness crosses the boundary between 'deviant' and 'natural' and exists as both. I further argue that medical social control (Foucault, 1973),[2] like other forms of social control, is exerted over trans people and serves to limit what healthcare they can access and how they can access it. In the second portion of the chapter, I look at possibilities for limiting or eliminating that medical social control, in other words I outline a proposal for demedicalization. Here I use the work of Georges Canguilhem and compare some of the problems with the demedicalization of homosexuality with the proposed demedicalization of transness. In spite of these challenges, I propose that a non-pathologizing model for transness is necessary and urgent.

Bureaucracy, time, and space

In Chapter 5 I expand upon the discussion of medical social control outlined in the previous chapter by analyzing some the mechanisms that are used to exert power over trans people. I start by looking at healthcare in the UK as a bureaucracy which illuminates the structure of gatekeeping and barriers that are placed between trans people and accessing the healthcare they need. The elements of these bureaucracies that the participants helped illuminate, including cancelled appointments, 'ticking boxes', jumping through hoops, shifting responsibility, the structure of forms, and social networks (Varela, 2001), are all sites in which trans people come up against barriers they must navigate to access their healthcare. I also look at time as a key factor in these power structures which particularly manifests as waiting. I use Brown et al's work on waiting for a liver transplant to unpack how waiting operates in a healthcare context and I consider some of the ways people deal with waiting, including an understanding of what makes waiting easier (Maister, 2005) and a more positive perspective on taking time (Israeli-Nevo, 2017). Finally, I look at the physical spaces in which trans people create and enact their gender, particularly waiting rooms and bathrooms, with the help of Lucas Crawford's work on transgender architecture. These spaces, time, and state and medical bureaucracies are simultaneously tools and loci of power which can keep trans people from maintaining or achieving health.

Pedagogy and TransLiteracy

In Chapter 6 I look at how trans communities use an alternative form of pedagogy, one that is social and decentralized, to exchange unique and targeted knowledges that I call TransLiteracy. I specifically highlight the ways in which trans people learn to strategically deploy personal narrative (Spade, 2000/2006; Latham, 2016), but I recognize a wide range of knowledges that are exchanged in this way. This includes everything from how to get referred to a gender identity clinic (GIC) to what shirts would be flattering: basically anything and everything a trans person may need to know in order to navigate the world. These knowledges are dispersed in different ways but I focus on social media as a key pedagogical tool. I use the early work of Mark Poster to understand the unique features of the internet that lead to it being such an important communication and narratological medium. Specifically, I investigate how trans people use YouTube (Raun, 2016), Facebook (Duguay, 2016), Instagram, and Twitter, and I show how this model is incredibly effective. Being decentralized decreases gatekeeping[3] and every participant in this information exchange can, at one point or another, act as both the teacher and the student, adding to or learning from the lived experience of these communities. Being social contextualizes and personalizes the information as well as providing a diverse range of voices, ensuring the person trying to learn has the best opportunity to get accurate and helpful answers to their questions. The social aspect of pedagogy along with specific trans knowledges such as understanding the trans dialect further help to build community. In this way, pedagogy and TransLiteracy help trans people overcome barriers to their health through becoming better able to access transition and non-transition related healthcare, getting advice that can help alleviate distress, and building community which bolster good mental health.

Language

Trans

The terminology used throughout this book can be difficult to definitively define. Different terms have been used to describe trans people throughout history and different people today use some of these terms in unique ways to define themselves. Any definitions I put forth are only relevant at a population level, as individual use of the same terms may vary greatly. For example, one interview participant does not identify as a trans man, he simply identifies as a man. However, he is still able to participate in this study because he falls under the trans umbrella when looked at from the broad view, or as he puts it, he is a "man with a trans history" (Adam). Using these umbrella terms is an imperfect way to tackle the necessary task of discussing a group of people without purporting to be able to label any individual within that group.

Transgender, meaning to cross over genders, can encompass anyone who blurs gender identity lines in one way or another. In other words, a transgender person is someone who has a gender identity different from the one usually associated with the sex they were assigned at birth. This is not the shortest way to explain this but I have chosen this language carefully to be as accurate as possible. Terms like 'born male' or 'natal gender' do not resonate with trans people who see themselves as having been born their true gender, just with a different than expected body. To say 'gender identity different from the gender assigned at birth' is not fully accurate as it is sex that is assigned at birth, generally based on the limited criteria of genital appearance, not gender. Saying 'gender identity different from the one usually associated with the sex they were assigned at birth' highlights the false deterministic relationship assigned to these two factors. I will go into this in more detail about this relationship in Chapters 2 and 3. The shortened version of transgender, trans, is also used as an adjective in combination with other words, for example the terms trans man and trans woman. I have no authority to give any of these existing terms a definitive definition nor to apply them to any individual, however I will be using trans throughout this book as a general term to discuss myself, the people who have participated in this study, and everyone else this work applies to. I will be using cisgender, or cis for short, to discuss everyone else who this text does not pertain to, that is, people who have a gender identity that is usually associated with the sex they were assigned at birth. An account of the changing umbrella terms for this community over time can be found in Mary Alice Adams' 2015 article, 'Traversing the Transcape: A Brief Historical Etymology of Trans Terminology'.

Other terminology

In addition to terminology specifically describing trans people, there is terminology in the upcoming sections that may be new to some readers outside trans communities or unfamiliar with the field of trans studies. I will define some of those terms as I will be using them here as a general guide for the reader, however, once again, these are not conclusive definitions. Language is constantly changing and different people may use or not use certain terms for themselves for various reasons. To this end, definitions of more specific gender identities are absent although their meaning and usage will be explored throughout the book in relation to the identities of interview participants. It is best practice to allow people to explain and describe their gender in their own words, which all informants for this research have been given space to do.

I have already mentioned cisgender. Essentially the opposite of the root trans, the Latin root cis means on this side of or on the same side of, so the term cis or cisgender refers to people who have a gender identity that matches the one usually associated with the sex they were assigned at birth, such as someone who was assigned female at birth and identifies as a woman. This terminology was first coined by biologist Dana Leland Defosse in 1994 to draw attention to the universality of gender identity and to the fact that it is not just trans people who have a gender identity and need language to describe it (Adams, 2015: 178).

I have also mentioned non-binary people. This is a term under the trans umbrella but is also an umbrella term itself. In the UK, and of course more broadly, babies are assigned one of two sexes at birth, male or female. Even babies who are neither of these two sexes are forced into one category or the other, which I will discuss further in the section on intersex people in Chapter 2. These two sexes are then conflated with genders to form the gender binary, the incorrect assumption that everyone is either male or female. Some trans people orient themselves within that binary, however some people are neither, both, shift around, have no gender, or have a completely different gender not related to male or female: the possibilities are vast. These people are who I am discussing when I use the term 'non-binary'.

Another way to categorize within the trans umbrella is with the terms transfeminine and transmasculine. Transfeminine can be used to describe AMAB (assigned male at birth) trans people and transmasculine to refer to AFAB (assigned female at birth) trans people. These are extremely useful terms for being able to include non-binary people. For example, when explaining who seeks testosterone, being able to say 'transmasculine people' rather than just 'trans men' is more accurate and inclusive. However, these terms come with their own set of problems. It creates a false connection between the relative femininity and masculinity of someone's gender identity in relation to the perceived relative femininity and masculinity of the sex they were assigned at birth. In this way the terms do not account for AMAB trans people who are and/or present in more masculine ways and AFAB trans people who are and/or present in more feminine ways as well as those people who are and/or present equally masculine and feminine or who may fit completely outside those concepts. The language becomes conflated because masculine and feminine and their counterparts male and female are used to in English to refer to sex and bodies, gender, clothing, other methods of gender expression, and social roles. The AMAB/AFAB framework is not ideal either, as it does not perfectly allow for intersex people. I will use transmasculine and transfeminine carefully throughout with the intention of being more inclusive of non-binary people, but if I were to say, for example, 'many transfeminine people seek estrogen', I am not implying anything about this group's bodies, gender roles, or gender expressions. I am simply trying to refer to all trans people who may want estrogen and cannot make enough of their own. It is my hope that as the language used in the field of trans studies and by trans communities continues to evolve that better and more accurate terminology will develop.

Transitioning is a term commonly used to discuss the process of 'changing' from one gender to another or as Ruth Pearce describes it: 'Transition refers to a move away from the gender that was assigned to a person at birth, and towards to an alternative preferred, desired or felt state of gendered (or non-gendered) being' (2018: 4). I will problematize this term and question its relevance later but this is how it is commonly used. There are also different categories of transitioning, such as social transition, which refers to people changing things like their name, pronouns, and outward gender expression, and medical transition, where people seek hormone replacement therapy and different surgical procedures in order to be more comfortable in their bodies. I will also differentiate between 'transition related healthcare' to refer to all healthcare needs that trans people have specifically because they are trans and 'non-transition related healthcare' to refer to all other healthcare needs they have that are not specifically trans related.

Passing is another relevant concept. This refers to being seen as a certain gender by most people most of the time. It is usually used in the context of trans people passing as their actual gender, for example a trans woman who is correctly gendered by strangers and who is not identified as trans by people who don't know her status is said to 'pass'. Although they were discussing intersex people,[4] American sociologist Harold Garfinkel defines someone's passing as 'the work of achieving and making secure their rights to live in the elected sex status while providing for the possibility of detection and ruin carried out within the socially structured conditions' (1967/2006: 60). So passing is that state which grants a trans person ease of movement through society but carries with it the specter of being 'found out'. People know they are passing based on different gendered social cues such as being called 'sir' or 'ma'am', the pronouns people use to talk about them, and not being questioned on their gender.

The scope of 'health'

As may already be apparent, what is considered to be relevant to trans health is considered very generously here. Of course there are those specific transition related healthcare needs such as hormones, a myriad of surgeries, gender-specific psychotherapy, and so on. Then there are the auxiliary health challenges that are unique to trans people but are not transition related such as men requiring pap smears and women who need prostate exams. Then there is every other healthcare need that any person could have in their lifetime but which can be complicated by someone's trans status. In his foreword to *Transgender Health: A Practitioner's Guide to Binary and Non-Binary Trans Patient Care*, Dr. Stuart Lorimer calls for all medical care providers to familiarize themselves with trans healthcare, saying '[w]e, as a profession, no longer have the luxury of treating trans as an esoteric little micro-speciality' (2018: 12) and 'it is the duty of every medical practitioner to manage gender-related issues safely and effectively' (2018: 13). Since trans people can have any health issue and require any specialism and treatment, it is crucial for all clinicians to expect to treat trans patients.

However, in addition to these individual healthcare needs, there are also public health factors to consider. Trans people are at a high risk for physical and sexual assault, murder, and suicide; they experience discrimination in education, housing, and employment, and they often lose close ties to friends, family, and community (see Kreiss and Patterson, 1997; Lombardi et al, 2002; Clements-Nolle et al, 2006; Badgett et al, 2007; Whittle et al, 2007; Stotzer, 2009; Bradford et al, 2013; Lee and Kwan, 2014; Talusan et al, 2016). All of these factors can lead to poor health outcomes (see Jin et al, 1995; Cutler and Lleras-Muney, 2006; Schanzer et al, 2007; Ryan et al, 2009; Yadegarfard et al, 2014). These indicators that impact trans people will be considered as part and parcel of health throughout this book. It is important to understand trans health beyond the framework of hormone therapy and surgeries as well as beyond the clinical encounter.

> [H]ealth is dependent upon not only good clinical care but also social and political climates that provide and ensure social tolerance, equality, and the full rights of citizenship. Health is promoted through public policies and legal reforms that promote tolerance and equity for gender and sexual diversity and that eliminate prejudice, discrimination, and stigma. (The World Professional Association for Transgender Health, 2012: 1–2)

I will employ this shift in focus throughout this book in order to give a broader and more informative view of trans health.

Healthcare in the UK

While not every healthcare interaction in the UK takes place within the NHS, it is the crux of the British medical system. Any changes made to private care would only impact the small number of people who can afford and choose those services and such changes would be decentralized while changes to the NHS have the potential to impact a much greater number as any resident is eligible to receive those services free at the point of care.[5] The fact that care provided on the NHS is publicly funded however may restrict clinicians' practices. As Bouman et al explain:

> [I]t is important to note that there is a key difference between privately and publicly funded health care. In the former, an absence of harm from treatment may be sufficient, provided the person accessing the intervention is making an informed decision. In the latter, there must be a demonstrable positive benefit of treatment for patients. This is because those paying for interventions for others (tax-payers) rightly expect their money to have been put towards some practical end and not merely be used to fulfil a desire on the part of the person seeking services. (Bouman et al, 2014: 378)

There are aspects of healthcare, including dental, eye care, and prescriptions, which are supplemented through taxation but do incur some cost to the individual at the point of care.

The history of the NHS is long and rich but here I will highlight only those few developments that are relevant to this book. In 2008, the concept of free choice was introduced, allowing patients who are seeking a referral from their General Practitioner (GP) for specialist care to choose any care provider or hospital that meets the NHS standards of care (Thorlby and Gregory, 2008). This means that trans people seeking a referral to a GIC from their GP do not have to be referred to the clinic that is geographically closest to them. I go into more detail around the process of making this choice in Chapter 4. In 2009 the health secretary pledged to eliminate 'mixed sex' hospital accommodation by the following year, thus making all accommodation 'single-sex' (Beasley and Flory, 2009). This was intended to ensure 'privacy' and 'dignity' but creates problems for trans people who want to be housed according to their gender identity and people who do not fit into binary sex and/or gender categories. Also in 2009 the NHS Constitution was published, outlining the rights patients have and what they should expect and demand from their health services. This includes a maximum 18-week wait time from the day you are referred by a GP to beginning specialist treatment (NHS, 2015). Currently, no GICs are meeting this standard, with the longest publicized wait time at the time of writing being just over seven years from referral to first appointment. In 2012 the Patient Choice Scheme was launched, as well as measures to increase the boundaries for GP practices (Department of Health, 2012). This means patients potentially have more GPs to choose from. For a trans person this is crucial, because if their request for a referral to a GIC is denied by one GP and/or they experience negative treatment from their practice, they have more GPs to choose from and can transfer and try again. Also in 2012 the NHS Mandate (applicable only to England) was first published. This mandate was updated in 2013 and is organized around the key areas of 'preventing people from dying prematurely', 'enhancing quality of life for people with long-term conditions', 'helping people to recover from episodes of ill health or following injury', 'ensuring that people have a positive experience of care', 'treating and caring for people in a safe environment and protecting them from avoidable harm', 'freeing the NHS to innovate', understanding 'the broader role of the NHS in society', 'finance', and 'assessing progress and providing stability' (Department of Health). I will examine how the NHS has achieved some of these standards in relation to trans people throughout this book.

Remits of the gender identity clinics

NHS England commissions[6] three components of service on what they call the 'gender dysphoria pathway'. These three components are the youth service which includes therapeutic and endocrinological care for people under the age of 18, gender clinics for adults 'offering assessment, diagnosis, overall care coordination, hormone treatments, voice and communication therapies and talking therapies', and surgical services for adults (Fairbairn et al, 2020).

The NHS has different service specifications for each of the three components of the gender dysphoria pathway: children services, adult non-surgical services, and adult surgical services. This work is focused on adults so experiences of the children's services will not be covered.

Non-surgical services for adults in the UK fall under the responsibility of the various GICs. Each GIC has a senior clinical lead that heads a multidisciplinary team with expertise in mental health and social support, endocrinology, voice and communication, trichology, administration, and generally all the health needs that someone accessing transition related healthcare may have. The specific non-surgical services offered can include talking therapy, HRT, facial hair removal, voice therapy, and support with social transition (NHS, nda).

Surgical interventions for adults are provided by specialist surgical teams, based in hospitals across the country. Surgical services are commissioned outside the structure of the GICs, although the GICs refer people to these surgical teams. If there is more than one team performing the required procedure, the individual can request which team they want to be referred to. Each surgical provider has a senior clinical lead that heads a multidisciplinary team with expertise in the particular surgical techniques they offer, anesthesiology, radiology, nursing, administration, and any other skills that are relevant to the procedures they perform. The procedures that are commissioned by the NHS fall under two categories, chest surgeries and genital surgeries. The standard chest procedures that are commissioned are double mastectomy (double incision or peri-areolar technique), masculinizing chest liposuction, nipple repositioning (including pedicled flaps), nipple grafting, nipple-areolar complex modification, dermal implant, and nipple tattooing. The standard genital procedures that are commissioned are various types of phalloplasty, metoidioplasty, urethroplasty, scrotoplasty including testicular prosthesis, hysterectomy, bilateral salpingo-oophorectomy, vaginectomy, placement of and training in the use of penile prosthesis, glans sculpting, penectomy, bilateral orchidectomy, vaginoplasty, clitoroplasty, and vulvoplasty. Procedures that are not routinely commissioned include phonosurgery, augmentation mammoplasty, facial feminization surgery, thyroid chondroplasty, rhinoplasty, lipoplasty/contouring, microdermabrasion, general 'cosmetic' procedures, body hair removal that is not on a surgical donor site, hair transplantation, or the reversal of any procedures accessed as part of the gender dysphoria pathway. Additionally, hysterectomy, bilateral salpingo-oophorectomy, penectomy, and orchidectomy are not commissioned as standalone procedures, therefore accessing any of these procedures without a concurrent phalloplasty, metoidioplasty, vaginoplasty, or vulvoplasty requires the approval of the individual's Clinical Commissioning Group for funding (NHS, ndb). If someone is seeking care that falls outside of the NHS specification they will have to either apply to their local CCG for funding or access it through a private provider.

Private healthcare

It is important to note that private healthcare continues to be an option for those who can afford it in the UK, and trans people know this option well. One of the main advantages of 'going private' as it is called is that the wait times are significantly shorter. For trans people who are struggling with long waiting lists to receive care (this is discussed at length in Chapter 5), going private can get them started on their transition sooner, something that can save lives. One participant, Dan, discussed how his NHS referral process was initially held up through some clerical errors. Once he was on the waiting list, he endured the estimated wait time he was initially quoted but still had not received a letter with an appointment date. When he was finally able to get a more realistic estimate for his first appointment date, which at that time was seven to eight months from the referral, he decided he could not wait that long.

> '[T]here was a complete meltdown and a re-evaluation cause at that point everything was being held back because I was gonna get seen

and something was gonna start moving and just the thought that it wasn't gonna be moving forward just kind of threw me into not a great place.' (Dan)

He reassessed his finances and sought private care. Within a month he was starting testosterone, a huge difference from people's experience getting hormones through the NHS. He went private for his double mastectomy as well, but the obvious downside to this is financial. Dan's initial consultation cost around £260, then there were four counseling appointments at £75 apiece, another £260 appointment, and £180 for a three-month supply of testosterone. Between the counseling required to access hormones, hormones themselves, and double mastectomy surgery, Dan estimates he is about £8,000 in debt. He is currently struggling with the wait for phalloplasty but says he absolutely has to go through the NHS for that because he cannot afford another private procedure. So while it is a costly option and a less common one, private healthcare is still a route some trans people take and is a factor to consider when trying to understand the full picture of trans healthcare in the UK.

1

Trans methodology

In this first chapter I explain the methodology, which I argue is itself a key finding of this research. I begin with outlining my ethical framework for a specifically trans methodology. This framework centers around four elements: that the research is done entirely within the communities; that if interviews are used they center the voices of trans people in their own words; that the research is written up in a trans style (which I describe in more detail later in this chapter); and that the research is disseminated back into the communities in an accessible way. This is a methodology that I hope to continue developing and improving throughout my career. I conclude the chapter by theorizing the role of autoethnography in trans studies generally and in this work specifically, using the work of Ellis, Boylorn and Orbe, Chang, Adams, Gergen and Gergen, and Jones to craft what I call an autoethnography of always.

Toward a trans methodology

One of the key aims of this book is to identify what ethics and practices might make up a specifically trans research methodology. I argue that the first feature of such a methodology is that the research is done entirely within the communities, which is to say that it is done by trans people.[1] It is my firm belief that the only ethical body of scholarship regarding a marginalized group can be constructed by and within that group. It is possible that there are exceptions to this rule but only by cis scholars who collaborate closely and fully with trans colleagues and have a deep reflexive understanding of their own privilege.[2] While not an exact corollary I am inspired by Black, indigenous, and other scholars of color researching and creating scholarship on race. In 'The Imperial Scholar: Reflections on a Review of Civil Rights Literature', legal scholar and one of the founders of critical race theory Richard Delgado states:

> While no one could object if sensitive white scholars contribute occasional articles and useful proposals (after all, there are many more of the mainstream scholars), must these scholars make a career of it? The time has come for white liberal authors who write in the field of civil rights to redirect their efforts and to encourage their colleagues to do so as well. There are many other important subjects that could

and should engage their formidable talents. As those scholars stand aside, nature will take its course; I am reasonably certain that the gap will quickly filled by talented and innovative minority writers and commentators. The dominant scholars should affirmatively encourage their minority colleagues to move in this direction, as well as simply to make the change possible. (Delgado, 1984: 577)

Here Delgado is calling not for white scholars to completely abandon the discipline, but rather to take responsibility for ushering in the new era of scholarship that centers scholars of color. Trans studies has already achieved a robust catalogue of work created by trans people, some of which is highlighted throughout this book. This work is theoretically rich and has moved the discipline into new and interesting places. It is in this tradition that the trans methodology that I propose would continue.

The second feature of a trans methodology requires interrogating the style of interview when this method is used. It is absolutely essential to center trans voices in their own words, thus interviews are a crucial medium for data gathering. Specifically, open-ended interviews that are unstructured or only loosely structured minimize the limiting effect that an interviewer's specific questions can have on what the interviewee says. In combination with the first tenet, the interview experience itself will be smoother because the participant will not need to educate the interviewer on 'trans 101' and the conversation and subsequent analysis will not be mediated through the cis gaze.[3] In addition to the benefits for the research, this interview style might be useful to the participants. The opportunity to speak for and about oneself is essential to creating one's own identity (see Chapter 5) and participating in this type of interview potentially allows interviewees the opportunity to construct personal narrative in whatever way is meaningful to them.

To recruit interviewees for this research, I publicized this by posting flyers in trans spaces in London including CliniQ, the trans sexual health clinic, and Open Barbers the queer barber shop. I also announced it at trans support groups and posted on trans Facebook groups. The interviews were very loosely structured. I began by asking all participants the same identifying information (age, race, pronouns, and gender) to get a better understanding of the makeup of my participant pool. It was important to this study to allow the participants to describe themselves in their own words, particularly when it came to their gender. I tried to encourage people to take as much time as they needed to describe their gender so they would not feel rushed or pressured into using only one or two words. I specifically asked them how they would 'describe' their gender and said something along the lines of 'however long that takes you to do' or 'take your time'. I would then explain to them that I was interested in their experiences with healthcare and would get them started by asking them to describe their most recent experience of accessing healthcare. When at different points in the interview they finished talking and I did not have any more follow-up questions based on what they had already told me, I would ask about their experiences with different healthcare providers including being misgendered in healthcare settings, with accessing transition related healthcare, particularly positive or negative experiences with the National Health Service or private healthcare, and how being trans impacted their health and healthcare. Of these I would only raise the topics that had not already come up in the interview. At the end of every interview I asked participants if they had anything else they wanted to tell me, in order to give them the opportunity to tell additional stories they had thought of. In some cases these were not strictly related to healthcare, such as with Flora who discussed their university course and Ben who talked about his filmmaking projects.

This methodology's third key feature is the style of writing. I use a gender-neutral pronoun throughout (I have chosen the singular 'they', a choice I go into detail about in the introduction) unless the person has told me that their pronouns are otherwise. I attempt to be cognizant of and to challenge biological essentialism and naturalization of 'gendered' traits at every turn. The writing style also includes weaving personal narrative in with theory (à la Paul B. Preciado's *Testo Junkie* [2013][4]). Most importantly, however, is how I write about the participants and their experiences. I do not approach them as though they themselves or their experiences are fixed. Rather, I see the interview as a snapshot of a moment in time that does not necessarily tell me anything about how these people have been or will be. I recognize the value in what they are able to relay without presuming that their experiences, opinions, identity, or anything else will remain fixed. If I went back to the same participants in a few years time it is very possible that some would identify their gender differently or that their perspective of the healthcare system would have become more positive or more negative. Indeed, the one participant who I was able to interview twice, Adam, consistently reported his gender simply as a 'man'. However, in the first interview he additionally described his gender experience as that of a 'transgender man' but said that he was somewhat uncomfortable with that term. In our second interview, about seven months later, Adam had found the term 'man with a trans history' which he felt suited him much better.

The final and perhaps most ethically important feature of a trans methodology is that the research products go back into the communities. A PhD or even an academic book as written products are inaccessible to the vast majority of people in trans communities, so this requires that the information be brought into trans spaces and actively made accessible. The next evolution of this ethic would be research that never truly leaves trans communities. Poet and trans studies scholar Lucas Crawford highlights the importance of this in their 2015 book *Transgender Architectonics: The Shape of Change in Modernist Space*: 'writing a theory of spatiality that presumes a transgender visitor to the space or transgender reader of this book is its own attempt to make new reading practices' (2015: 163). So perhaps in future, rather than doing insider community research, bringing it back to the academy to analyze and disseminate, and then bringing accessible results to communities, every stage of the research would take place within and in conversation with trans communities. This would fundamentally challenge the role of the university in this type of research or perhaps reshape the boundaries of the university itself.

Dynamic methodologies

This methodology was not one that was decided on in advance of this project and then put into practice, but rather came about during and as a result of the project. Therefore several adaptations were made in the process of writing this research, such as shifting from using trans★ as an umbrella term, which was still commonly deployed when I first proposed this project in 2015 but had mostly fallen out of use a few years later. Another example is that the interviews became increasingly less structured as it became apparent that the interviewees knew the stories that were relevant to them and did not need much guidance beyond a general conversation topic. It is in this spirit that I acknowledge that the minutiae of the trans methodology that I have outlined may change, in fact that it must change, in the future guided by the communities being researched.

Other minority studies

This trans methodology has been heavily influenced by general trends across minority studies, specifically those within critical race theory (CRT)/critical race studies (CRS), disability studies, and fat studies.[5] As I will outline in the following sections, each of these bodies of literature share several traits with this trans methodology. These include conducting research completely within communities, interdisciplinarity,[6] and privileging the first-hand accounts of people within those communities. Each of them provides a useful framework for researching specific marginalized minority groups.

Critical race theory

Just as this trans methodology advocates an applied approach, CRT includes an important activist element. It is collaborative and community based, or as Delgado and Stefancic describe in *Critical Race Theory: An Introduction*, it is 'a collection of activists and scholars engaged in studying and transforming the relationship among race, racism, and power' (2017: 3). This distinguishes

CRT from civil rights discourse in that it is focused on questioning and reimagining entire systems rather than on making incremental progress toward achieving equal rights. The basic tenets of CRT recognize that 'racism is ordinary, not aberrational' (Delgado and Stefancic, 2017: 8), that white supremacy benefits white people and serves important social, cultural, and symbolic purposes for them, and that race is a social construct. These tenets are rooted in valuing and validating the lived experiences of Black people and other people of color, which is similar to the aims of this trans methodology with regard to trans people. CRT also recognizes and values intersectionality and supports the 'voice-of-color thesis'.

> [T]he voice-of-color thesis holds that because of their different histories and experiences with oppression, black, Indian, Asian, and Latino/a writers and thinkers may be able to communicate to their white counterparts matters that whites are unlikely to know. Minority status, in other words, brings with it a presumed competence to speak about race and racism. (Delgado and Stefancic, 2017: 11)

I would be remiss to simply replace the voice-of-color thesis with something like a 'voice-of-trans' thesis because being a person of color and being trans are in no way analogous, as I explain in what follows. Indeed the voice-of-color thesis could be added to this methodology by a trans person of color in order to study their own communities. However, the idea of the voice-of-color thesis has strongly inspired the first (the research is done entirely within the communities) and second (if interviews are used they center the voices of trans people in their own words) elements of this trans methodology. In addition to these similarities, CRT and trans studies generally share an interdisciplinary approach. While CRT has its disciplinary roots in law schools and legal studies, over the last few decades it has also become important to social science and humanities disciplines. As Angela Harris explains in the foreword to *Critical Race Theory: An Introduction*, '[c]ritical race theory has exploded from a narrow sub-specialty of jurisprudence chiefly of interest to academic lawyers into a literature read in departments of education, cultural studies, English, sociology, comparative literature, political science, history, and anthropology around the country' (2017: xvi).[7] This ability to not only speak across disciplines but to use the strengths and insights of diverse disciplines to one's advantage as a researcher is crucial to the trans methodology that I outline in this chapter.

Disability studies

This trans methodology highlights the importance of researchers who have lived experience of the area they are researching and showcases other voices from within the communities being researched. Both of these methodological strategies are also applicable to disability studies. James Charlton describes their approach to writing their book *Nothing About Us Without Us: Disability Oppression and Empowerment* as one of foregrounding the first-hand experience of disability, both their own and that of others:

> This book is founded principally on the everyday life of people with disabilities. It derives first and foremost from my own particular experiences as a person with a disability and as an activist in the disability rights movement in the United States. Second, it comes out of others' experiences described in conversations, discussions, and interviews or excerpted from the existing literature. (Charlton, 2000: 5)

Here Charlton describes lived experience as foundational, whether it be accessed from the personal experience of the author, from interviews and conversations with other community members, from existing literature, or in their case (as in mine), all of the above. They also specifically mention their activism. It is not only notable that they are coming to this writing as a person with a disability, but also that they are bringing their perspective and experience as a disability rights activist to research, methodology, and theorization. Finally, disability studies and this trans methodology are concerned with challenging what constitutes a 'normal' embodiment. As Lennard J. Davis states in the introduction to *The Disability Studies Reader*, 'the "problem" of disability does not lie with the person with disabilities but rather in the way that normalcy is constructed' (2016: 1). This eye toward unpacking and dismantling oppressive ideas of normalcy is an important factor of this methodology.

Fat studies

Following the fields of study already mentioned, another source of inspiration for this trans methodology comes from the field of fat studies. As Rothblum and Solovay explain in their introduction to *The Fat Studies Reader*, 'in the tradition of critical race studies, queer studies, and women's studies, fat studies is an interdisciplinary field of scholarship marked by an aggressive, consistent, rigorous critique of the negative assumptions, stereotypes, and stigma placed on fat and the fat body' (2009: 2). Fat studies represents yet another meeting point between academia and activism, the nexus of which is a building block of this trans methodology. In their foreword to *The Fat Studies Reader*, author and fat activist Marilyn Wann describes fat studies as 'a radical field, in the sense that it goes to the root of weight-related belief systems' (2009: ix). This is precisely how I view trans studies and this trans methodology. It is a radical endeavor, to borrow Wann's phrasing, to go to the root of gender-related belief systems and to disrupt prevailing societal understandings by highlighting the lived experiences of a marginalized minority group.

Additionally, both this trans methodology and the fat studies approaches described here challenge the medicalization of human diversity, particularly diversity of the human body. As Wann describes, 'medicalizing diversity inspires a misplaced search for a "cure" for naturally occurring difference' (2009: xiii). I launch a similar critique against the medicalization of transness in Chapter 4, where I argue for the demedicalization of transness while looking at how to retain access to necessary medical technologies. Fat studies approaches also question the usefulness of 'objectivity'. Wann argues that because we all live in a systemically fatphobic society, no researcher could possibly be completely objective in their analysis of fat people and fat bodies, regardless of their own position within that system. Furthermore, they state that 'claims of neutrality or objectivity in fat studies risk making analyses less credible, not more so' (2009: xviii). I apply this statement equally to trans studies, because, similarly, everyone has an experience with and relationship to gender which makes complete objectivity an impossibility. This is part of what led to the high value that I place on the roles of insider researchers, and to my decision to include autoethnography in the research.

Differentiating a trans methodology

Despite the inspiration and areas of overlap, this trans methodology remains distinct from any of the approaches discussed thus far. The key differentiating factor is the group that is being foregrounded. Highlighting trans identity as the subject of inquiry differentiates this approach, making it distinct from the approaches listed previously as well as from other queer studies approaches which privilege sexual orientation. This is because there are important differences in the experiences of different minority and marginalized groups which must, in turn, necessitate different research approaches.[8] For example, despite many ethical and methodological similarities, CRS and critical disability studies cannot be understood as perfectly analogous because of the different experiences of people of color and disabled people and the different ways in which racism and ableism operate. Additionally, some people fall into both minority groups and have unique experiences and challenges. In this example, those unique experiences necessitated the development of a new approach, dis/ability critical race studies (or DisCrit), to analyze that particular intersection (Annamma et al, 2012). Similarly, there could be an endless number of approaches developed which modify this trans methodology in order to research and evaluate the intersections of transness and any number of other marginalized experiences. Because this is a methodology that foregrounds trans people and transness as the singular subjects of research, most of the elements of this methodology are trans specific. This necessitates the highlighting of trans people's voices, using a trans writing style (as described in this chapter), and disseminating the research findings back into trans communities in ways that are specifically tuned to the needs of those communities (for example via presentations in accessible language at trans meet-ups).

Limitations

Any study of a community will struggle with the definition of that community's boundaries, and with this methodology that challenge comes on two fronts. Both the researcher and the participants must be able to understand themselves as belonging to some kind of shared community and/or having a common set of lived experiences. As I have already addressed, selecting an umbrella term for the communities that are being researched (and to which the researcher belongs) is necessary to understand who is included and excluded in this research, although this creates its own problems. Potential participants who do not identify with that umbrella term may not participate in the research and thus the researcher will miss out on those perspectives. I have addressed this by using the most prevalent umbrella term in use at the time of writing ('trans'), explaining in recruitment material that this includes non-binary people, and recognizing that there is no perfect umbrella term that all potential participants will identify with so I will always miss some people. Umbrella terms also change so the research could seem out of date, potentially quite quickly, which is why it is important to note that this research is very specifically situated in the UK in the mid to late 2010s.

Autoethnography

In addition to the experiences I learned about through interviewing other trans people I also gained knowledge from my own experiences through autoethnography, which is the application of self-reflection on personal experiences to broader (in this case) sociological themes and theories. When describing the task of autoethnographers, Carolyn Ellis, a scholar whose body of work has focused on creative qualitative research methods and storytelling, explains that 'first they look through an ethnographic wide angle lens, focusing outward on social and cultural aspects of their personal experience; then, they look inward, exposing a vulnerable self that is moved by and may move through, refract, and resist cultural interpretations' (2004: 37). Autoethnography is not unidirectional but requires a constant back and forth process of reference – both between the personal and the theoretical and between the individual and the community – that I have incorporated into this work.

On a very basic level, autoethnography can be described as using the lens of one's own lived experience to study sociocultural phenomena, what Boylorn and Orbe call 'cultural analysis through personal narrative' (2016: 17). Each of those two factors, cultural analysis and personal narrative, must be present to have autoethnography. Cultural analysis without personal narrative is just traditional ethnography. Equally, personal narrative without cultural analysis is simply autobiography. As Heewon Chang explains in *Autoethnography as Method*, '[s]temming from the field of anthropology, autoethnography shares the storytelling feature with other genres of self-narrative but transcends mere narration of self to engage in cultural analysis and interpretation' (2016: 43). Chang goes on to explain that 'autoethnography should be ethnographic in its methodological orientation, cultural in its interpretive orientation, and autobiographical in its content orientation' (2016: 48). This is the combination of elements I have employed as part of this work.

Why autoethnography?

Chang describes three main benefits of autoethnography: that 'it offers a research method friendly to researchers and readers', that 'it enhances cultural understanding of self and others', and that 'it has a potential to transform self and there to motivate them to work toward cross-cultural coalition building' (2016: 52).[9] As for myself, I was first drawn to autoethnography through a discomfort with trying to speak for people with vastly different lived experiences from my own, particularly those who experience oppression that I do not experience. As Tony Adams describes in *Autoethnography: Understanding Qualitative Research*, '[a]s a researcher, I am confident about my right (and privilege!) to speak for myself, but I am less confident about my right to speak on behalf of others' (Adams et al, 2015: 12). Rather than going out to study an 'other', autoethnography allows a researcher to give others (readers) a glimpse into their world. It 'is predicated on the ability to invite readers into the lived experience of a presumed "Other" and to experience it viscerally' (Boylorn and Orbe, 2016: 15). The value of giving readers that visceral experience is crucial for a project such as this that serves not only as educational material but also as a call to action.

I have specifically incorporated autoethnography into this work because, as a critical method, it is particularly useful for understanding systems of power and oppression and illuminating ways for addressing those systems. As Boylorn and Orbe note: 'We talk about autoethnography as a critical method by using three central features of critical theory, which include: to understand the lived experience of real people in context, to examine social conditions and uncover oppressive power arrangements, and to fuse theory and action to challenge processes of domination' (2016: 20). As these three features were already aims of the project as a whole, autoethnography was a perfect fit. The use of autoethnography also impacts the way the work is written. My use of autoethnography in this work has greatly influenced the trans writing style I have employed; as Gergen and Gergen describe in 'Ethnographic Representation as Relationship': 'In using oneself as an ethnographic exemplar, the researcher is freed from the traditional conventions of writing. One's unique voicing—complete with colloquialisms, reverberations from multiple relationships, and emotional expressiveness—is honored. In this way the reader gains a sense of the writer as a full human being' (2002: 14).

Similarly, in *The Blackwell Encyclopedia of Sociology*, Stacy Holman Jones describes autoethnographic outputs as texts that 'feature concrete action, are reflexive and self-critical, and strive to create an emotionally and intellectually charged engagement of selves, bodies, texts, and contexts' (2007: 231, original emphasis). By making the most of the emotive and conversational writing style that is achieved with autoethnography I hope to convey my findings in a way that connects with the reader and incites them to engage with the topic.

An autoethnography of always

Many of the insights that I have found particularly valuable throughout this research come from the fact that as a member of the group I am researching I share many of the experiences the participants are describing. In order to position myself as an insider researcher.[10] I found it necessary to acknowledge and gain knowledge from my own experience as a trans person. In doing so I am following a common disciplinary practice. In *Understanding Trans Health: Discourse, Power and Possibility*, British trans studies scholar Ruth Pearce notes that 'expertise was historically located not simply in the medical professions, but also within the detached perspective of non-trans writers' (2018: 31). Similarly, in 'Mutilating Gender', American legal scholar and trans activist Dean Spade recognizes that '[in] most writing about trans people, our gender performance is put under a microscope to prove theories or build "expertise" while the gender performances of the authors remain unexamined and naturalized' (2000/2006: 316). The mere fact of my being a trans person writing about trans people does not inherently avoid this pitfall. However, by specifically addressing my own experience with and relationship to gender alongside the experiences of the participants I hope to produce a work that is collaborative rather than exploitative. In the Introduction to 'Mutilating Gender' in the *Transgender Studies Reader*, Susan Stryker and Stephen Whittle remark that Spade's 'refusal to feign a disinterested distance from the topic of his analysis, his explicit articulation of his embodied stake in the matter at hand, and the knowledge gained from his own embodied situation all exemplify important methodological hallmarks of transgender studies' (2006: 315). Following them, Australian trans health scholar J.R. Latham states that 'trans studies as a critical field insists on the author taking account of oneself … the very emergence of trans studies hinges on explicitly prioritising the work of trans people and taking our experiences seriously' (2017: 180–181). Like Latham, I understand this practice within the framework of autoethnography but with a unique application. What I offer here is not an autoethnographic perspective of a specific moment, event, or trauma. It is an autoethnography of always. It is about what I have experienced in the past, throughout and as a result of going through the process of this research, and my hopes for the future. It means when the participants describe their experiences to me, they land with additional emphasis because I have experienced the same or similar things or can imagine with clarity the possibility of those things happening to me. I am also able to write about these experiences with that same clarity which benefits the reader. The participants have certainly illuminated new perspectives and experiences beyond what I would be able to personally share, but nevertheless my understanding of these concepts comes from a place of close proximity.

I made the decision not to separate out the autoethnographic component into its own chapter or into separate sections within the chapters because my experience is not any more interesting or important than that of anyone else. I aim to treat my own narratives in similar ways to those of other participants in this study and have woven my experiences throughout when they are relevant, as I have done with the experiences of the other participants. The interviews informed by the trans methodology outlined here and these autoethnographic elements combine to form the rich data set that will be referenced throughout the rest of this book.

2

Models of sex and gender

> [T]he task of distinguishing sex from gender becomes all the more difficult once we understand that gendered meanings frame the hypothesis and the reasoning of those biomedical inquiries that seek to establish 'sex' for us as it is prior to the cultural meanings that it acquires.
>
> Butler (1990: 148–149)

In this chapter, I will explore existing models for sex and gender in order to challenge those modes of understanding, particularly in how they influence medical understandings of identity and embodiment. Much of the conversation around validating trans people focuses on the difference between sex and gender[1] as concepts and on challenging the limited, binary definition of those two terms (Valdes, 1995). Sex is often framed in a heavily gendered way, contributing to a pervasive belief that sex and gender are interchangeable and that sex determines gender. Therefore by clearly separating gender from sex the connection that gender has to the physical is called into question or even disavowed, thus seemingly accounting for trans existence. Judith Butler sums this stance up thusly: 'Originally intended to dispute the biology-is-destiny formulation the distinction between sex and gender serves the argument that whatever biological intractability sex appears to have, gender is culturally constructed: hence, gender is neither the causal result of sex nor as seemingly fixed as sex' (1990: 8).

For example, I may have a 'female' body and have been assigned the female sex at birth, but because gender and sex are separate concepts my masculine gender identity can be validated in its separateness from my sex.[2] However, this separation promotes narratives that fail to accurately describe the diverse experiences of trans people. In this chapter I will argue that the best model for understanding sex and gender is in fact to understand them together, as deeply entwined concepts that constantly co-create each other. I unpack how sex is already understood through the lens of gender and the different problematic models for transness which that understanding leads to. This is not an argument to do away with the concept of gender altogether, but by understanding that sex is just as socially constructed and self-identified as gender and how gender and sex influence each other we can better understand the diversity of the embodied human experience.[3]

The egg and the sperm

The way physical bodies are discussed by medical professionals may appear to be an objective description of reality. However, anatomy and physiology textbooks are not immune to influence from the culture in which they were produced. Social scientists such as Emily Martin have challenged and analyzed the ways in which culture influences science and medicine. This influence is especially clear with scientific discussions of bodies and body parts that are strongly gendered, a perfect example being sex cells.

Martin has addressed this topic in 'The Egg and the Sperm: How Science Has Constructed a Romance Based on Stereotypical Male-Female Roles' (1991). This feminist critique specifically zeroes in on gametes as a prime example of the way the gendered body is represented and described in scientific literature. As Martin puts it, '[i]n the course of my research I realized that the picture of egg and sperm drawn in popular as well as scientific accounts of reproductive biology relies on stereotypes central to our cultural definitions of male and female' (1991: 485). In scientific literature, sperm cells are cast in the role of the brave and daring knight and the egg cell as the damsel in distress, or conversely the egg cell as the femme fatale and the sperm cell as her hapless victim. The metaphors and language used influence the supposedly objective scientific knowledge that is being conveyed. In this example, it was previously thought that the egg played no active role in fertilization, that this 'feminine' cell was passive and the 'masculine' sperm cells did all the hard work. Biologist and gender scholar Anne Fausto-Sterling noticed the same phenomenon when looking at the history of scientists trying to understand and classify sex hormones: 'social belief systems weave themselves into the daily practice of science in ways that are often invisible to the working scientist … gender and science form a system that operates as a single unit—for better and for worse' (2000: 194). Martin is arguing the latter, that this system creates biases that are detrimental to knowledge production. Much more is now known about fertilization and the active role the egg cell plays, and yet that picture can still be lost because of the continued use of gendered language by researchers when describing their findings. They are unable to break away from, firstly, the idea that egg cells are feminine and sperm cells are masculine, and, secondly, that this relates to cultural tropes of femininity as weak and passive and masculinity as strong and active, even to the detriment of scientific accuracy and knowledge production. This highlights the way in which biomedical knowledge cannot be extricated from the culture in which it is produced. Martin hopes that shining a light on the problematic nature of these gendered metaphors will not only improve our understanding of biological processes but 'will rob them of their power to naturalize our social conventions about gender' (Martin, 1991: 501).

While a discussion of transness is absent in Martin's work, I am expanding upon these ideas to better understand how trans people are impacted by the gendering of bodies and body parts. Sperm and egg cells being discussed in this gendered way further reinforces the idea that people who produce sperm cells are men and/or masculine and people who are born with egg cells are women and/or feminine. This is a particularly important biological stance to unpack as this is one trait that trans people are not yet able to change. For example, some trans women and other transfeminine people will cease to produce sperm cells, but they will not have egg cells as this is beyond the scope of current medical technology. In the popular and essentialist understanding of female bodies as ones that have egg cells (and everything that may go along with that, such as menstruation, pregnancy, et cetera.), transfeminine people's absence of sperm cells is overshadowed by their lack of egg cells. Trans men and other transmasculine people may have their ovaries and therefore their egg cells removed but again they are not able to produce sperm cells.[4] This leads to the use of terms such as male-bodied and female-bodied and the concepts of a people being born in and/or trapped in a 'male' or 'female' body. These terms and concepts rely on that differentiation between sex and gender, validating trans people's gender by saying that their gender and sex do not match. Philosopher Talia Mae Bettcher explains this phenomenon as such:

> In what I call the 'wrong-body' model, transsexuality involves a misalignment between gender identity and the sexed body. This idea developed in the context of sexology, medicine, and psychiatry (facilitated by technological developments). While in the psychological variant of the model, transsexuality is viewed as a problem of the mind (albeit treatable through sex reassignment surgery) by the medical establishment, in the wrong-body model proper, transsexuality is viewed as a problem of the body by transsexuals themselves. The wrong-body model proper has two versions. In the weak version, one is born with the medical condition of transsexuality and then, through genital reconstruction surgery, becomes a woman or a man (in proper alignment with an innate gender identity). In the strong version, one's real sex is determined by gender identity. On the basis of this native identity one affirms that one has always really been the woman or a man that one claims to be. In both versions, one is effectively a man or woman 'trapped in the wrong body'. (Bettcher, 2014: 383)

Under this model, a trans person's gender may be what they say it is, but their sex is something physical that remains unchanged. That, for example, despite being a woman a trans woman is 'biologically male', is trapped in that 'male body', and necessarily seeks to alter it. The narratives that I discuss throughout this section are problematic only at the population level. An individual may find strong identification with any or all of these narratives. The issues that I discuss here only arise when these narratives are applied to all trans people as a blanket explanation of our experience and identity.

Challenging the narrative

One way to challenge the 'wrong-body' narrative is by deconstructing the idea of the gendered body. While it is possible that this narrative has been a necessary stepping stone toward greater trans acceptance, as trans voices are increasingly present in the discussion, that story of being trapped in the wrong body is being disrupted. Whatever benefits have come from the sex/gender distinction, it also creates its own problem. The medicalized model of transness relies on this narrative in diagnosing gender dysphoria and 'treating' trans patients with hormone therapy and surgery, and:

> while most theorists appreciate that the medical system's recognition of gender variance has its benefits (e.g., access to safe treatments and surgeries, insurance coverage), they also acknowledge the ways in which this system reifies a dyadic and rigid view of gender and denigrates bodies that cannot be neatly organized into one of the two conventional gender categories: masculine male and feminine female. (Johnson and Repta, 2012: 33)

So this 'wrong-body' narrative still conflates sex and gender despite claiming to separate them. It allows for an understanding of gender that is not determined by sex, however it says that there is a certain body that is male and a certain body that is female and trans people will aspire to one of those bodies based on their gender identity. This turns the 'sex determines gender' narrative on its head because here gender determines sex as trans people are seen to be aligning their bodies with their gender. One of the problems with this model is that it changes the direction of influence from sex determining gender to gender determining sex without doing anything to challenge the status quo of those linked binaries. While I do hold that gender can influence sex, understanding gender as the sole and direct determiner of sex is overly simplistic and any model of sex and gender that only allows for two equated binaries (man and a 'male body' on one end and woman and a 'female body' on the other), regardless of the direction of influence, is woefully incomplete.

Sexual intermediaries

Dr. Magnus Hirschfeld's pioneering 1910 work, *The Transvestites: The Erotic Drive to Cross-Dress*, reads in many ways as far ahead of its time. It espouses many of the same ideas and offers similar recommendations to contemporary trans studies literature. It is in this work that Hirschfeld proposes the theory of sexual intermediaries to explain human sexual diversity. 'By sexual intermediaries we understand ... and their number is not limited ... ones who stand, in the physical or mental view, between a complete manly man and, in every respect, a womanly woman' (Hirschfeld, 1910/ 2006: 35). This intermediariness could be in one, several, or all four of the following categories: the sexual organs; the other physical characteristics; the sex drive; and the other emotional characteristics. We still use these same four categories today only we may call them genitalia and other reproductive organs, secondary sexual characteristics, sexual orientation, and gender identity.

Variations in the sexual organs accounts for the diversity that is intersex people (Hirschfeld used the term hermaphrodite). Variation in other physical characteristics include people assigned female at birth who grow beards and people assigned male at birth with pronounced breast tissue. These characteristics can be linked to being intersex as well but not in every case. Variations in sex drive would result in people who are asexual, homosexual, bisexual, or otherwise non-heterosexual. Hirschfeld further includes people who transgress traditional gender roles in their sex lives, for example, men who enjoy being submissive and women who like to dominate. Variations in the final category of other emotional characteristics are where this work is primarily focused. This category includes trans and other gender non-conforming people.

People can of course encompass any or all of these variations in different ways and to different degrees. The possibilities for diversity are endless. Hirschfeld even questioned if it was possible to not have any of these variations whatsoever.

> Accordingly, a complete womanly and 'absolute' woman would be such a one who not only produces egg cells but also corresponds to the womanly type in every other respect; an 'absolute' man would be such a one who forms semen cells yet also, at the same time, exhibits the manly average type in all other points. These kinds of absolute representatives of their sex are, however, first of all only abstractions, invented extremes; in reality they have not as yet been observed, but rather we have been able to prove that in every man, even if only to a small degree, there is his origin from the woman, in every woman the corresponding remains of manly origins. (Hirschfeld, 1910/2006: 35)

Here Hirschfeld is claiming that in fact no one is free from variations in these categories. While perhaps people who have enough variation in any one category to identify themselves (or be labeled) with a particular identity are in the minority, the experience of diversity within sex and gender is a fundamentally human one.

This represented a radical shift in sexology and the as yet undefined field of trans studies. Hirschfeld maintains that there is something inherent about masculinity and femininity while completely divorcing those concepts from having any explicit link to biological sex, gender identity, sexual orientation, or gender expression. This allows for the validation of endlessly diverse genders, sexes, sexual orientations, and any combination thereof.

Intersex

The existence of intersex people refutes these sex binaries. One of the first orders of business after a baby is born is to tick off 'm' or 'f' on the basis of genital appearance, but with some intersex babies that is not possible. For other intersex people who did have a clear 'm' or 'f' assignment at birth, some become aware of being intersex later in life and indeed some people may never know they are intersex. Intersex people have characteristics used to determine sex, mainly genital appearance, the internal reproductive system, hormone secretion, and the 23rd chromosomal pair, which do not all fit into the same one of two boxes. This can manifest in many different ways but some of the possibilities are: androgen insensitivity syndrome where people have XY chromosomes but develop 'female' external genitalia; congenital adrenal hyperplasia where people have XX chromosomes but increased androgen production leading to genitalia that appears 'male'; Klinefelter syndrome where someone who is usually assigned male has an extra X chromosome (XXY); Turner syndrome where someone usually assigned female is missing an X chromosome (X); and Rokitansky syndrome where people are usually assigned female based on their XX chromosomes and external genitalia but have a shorter vagina and no cervix or womb (NHS, 2023). All of these ways of being intersex show that sex is more complicated than a simple male–female binary.

Biological sex is clearly more than just 'male' and 'female', but the sex binary is so deeply ingrained that standard practice since the relevant medical technology has been available has been to perform genital surgery on infants, as described by gynecologist Sarah Creighton in the *Journal of the Royal Society of Medicine*:

> Clinicians aim to choose the gender that carries the best prognosis for reproductive and sexual function and for which the genitalia and physical appearance can be made to look most normal. It is thought this will ensure a stable gender identity. If surgery is required, it is performed as soon as possible and no later than 24 months. (Creighton, 2001: 218)

In their 2006 article 'Consensus Statement on Management of Intersex Disorders', Hughes et al further illuminated the perceived need for expediency as well as the criteria used to make the gender assignment:

> Initial gender uncertainty is unsettling and stressful for families. Expediting a thorough assessment and decision is required. Factors that influence gender assignment include the diagnosis, genital appearance, surgical options, need for life long replacement therapy, the potential for fertility, views of the family, and sometimes the circumstances relating to cultural practices. (Hughes et al, 2006: 556)

This is a multitude of diverse factors and itself complicates any notion that sex identification is a straightforward matter. The input of the parents and even cultural practices (they later allude to the stigma in certain cultures around female infertility) are cited here as medically valid reasons to commence medical procedures that in adulthood would be considered 'sex reassignment' or a medical gender transition. The gender identity and wishes of the individual are notably absent as factors on assigning the 'sex of rearing' as it is called in many of these documents. Even convenience factors are addressed, with Hughes et al stating that 'feminising as opposed to masculinising genitoplasty requires less surgery to achieve an acceptable outcome and results in fewer urological difficulties' (2006: 558). A key problem is that this is framed as an immediate issue requiring immediate intervention, and so the individual may be too young to have formed a gender identity or to be consulted.

The theme throughout the medical literature on intersex people is that having an intersex variation is definitely a problem. 'If the appearance of the external genitalia is sufficiently ambiguous to render sex assignment impossible or the phenotype is not consistent with prenatal genetic tests, then de facto, extensive investigation is required' (Ahmed et al, 2011: 14). There is no interrogation here as to why not being able to easily tick 'm' or 'f' on the birth certificate is so distressing. Why is it that rather than conceive of a third or many more sexes these infants are operated on to fit their body into a narrow box? Or, as American philosopher and gender scholar Judith Butler asks, 'are these bodies subjected to medical machinery that marks them for life precisely because they are "inconceivable"?' (2001/2006: 187). Creighton goes on to unpack a lot of the controversy surrounding this practice and shows how the tides were beginning to change for the treatment of intersex infants in the early 2000s.

> Until lately, genital surgery has been seen as the mainstay of treatment but recent evidence suggests that this is not so. Adult patients are unhappy and feel mutilated and damaged by surgery performed on

them as young children, however worthy the clinician's motives. Although the technology for investigation and diagnosis of these conditions is improving rapidly with advances in biochemical and genetic testing, there are still few long-term data on the results of intervention. Clinicians working in this field must step back and review their practice. Surgery may not be necessary. We need much more information to allow clinicians and parents to make informed decisions, and for this purpose multicentre research on long-term outcomes is essential. (Creighton, 2001: 219–220)

Hughes et al recognize that 'medical interventions and negative sexual experiences may have fostered symptoms of post-traumatic stress disorder' and that intersex people may very well present as a gender different from the one chosen for them once they are old enough for gender identity to emerge (2006: 558).

These early surgical interventions are still performed in the UK. The literature that is linked to by the National Health Service for parents of intersex children walks them through the entire process of diagnosis, dealing with friends and family, psychological support, and so on but stops just short of explaining the actual treatment guidelines and how they can expect to navigate that process (Achermann and Achermann, 2014). Nonconsensual genital surgeries are still being performed on children, however, activism by intersex people has led to an increased awareness of the harm of this practice among medical professionals. Liao et al address this in a 2015 *British Medical Journal* article calling for a review of surgical interventions and the formation of non-surgical care paths. They note that 'gender assignment has become less simplistic but normalising surgery remains common' and specifically that 'the rate of female assigned and surgically feminised children who reassign as male is of concern' (Liao et al, 2015). There is definitely overlap with a discussion of trans health here, for example, those 'surgically feminized children' who identify as male may have a trans experience. The two groups are also undergoing many of the same 'treatments' including genital reconstruction surgeries and Hormone Replacement Therapy.

These surgical interventions for intersex children are permissible under current UK law because parents have been granted the legal right to consent by proxy. Infants are by definition unable to give consent to any procedure. Further, the particular procedures I am discussing here are neither medically necessary nor time sensitive. Thus there is no need to perform them before the individual is old enough to give informed consent. This understanding of these procedures – as nonconsensual – comes from a human rights perspective which may be used as a basis to challenge current law (Garland and Slokenberga, 2019). This push for reform in how intersex infants and children are treated is supported by the demedicalization perspective proposed in Chapter 4.

Beyond the binary

Non-binary people also inherently disrupt the 'wrong-body' narrative. If there is no conception of an ideal non-binary body, then how are non-binary people 'trapped' in their current body and what type of body are they supposed to be aspiring to?[5] There can be no 'wrong-body' narrative without the accompanying 'right body'. I am not trapped in my body, if I am trapped in anything it is in a world that doesn't make room for me and I wholly reject any notion that being trans means I have to hate my body. Of course some trans people do hate or have an otherwise complicated relationship to their body and this is not to dismiss that experience but rather to open up further possibilities. In his work with transmasculine people in Australia, J.R. Latham identifies four axioms that typify the way medical texts and even seemingly supportive medical care providers conceive of transness. They are that '1) transexuality is a disjuncture between mind and body; 2) transexuality is hating having the wrong genitals; 3) transexuality is painful and debilitating; and 4) transexuality is resolvable with surgical and hormonal body modifications' (Latham, 2016: 30). These ideas, that trans people have a disconnect between their psychological gender and their physical body, which leads them to hate that body causing them extreme distress that can only be relieved by medical intervention bringing the mind and body back into alignment, are the institutional codification of the 'wrong-body' narrative. It is this model that defines trans people in relation to the necessary hatred of their bodies that many trans people are resisting.[6]

It is perfectly reasonable for a trans person to feel uncomfortable in their body and/or wish to change it, but change is certainly not necessary and it is not what defines us as being trans. I do not see my body as female despite the 'F' marker that appears on my birth certificate. My experience inside this body is as a transmasculine non-binary person and this body that has carried me through that lived experience is also masculine and non-binary regardless of any of its individual features. I, like most people, could not even identify most of those features with any degree of certainty. I have never had my chromosomes tested, I have never seen my internal reproductive system, and I don't need to. It would not change my gendered experience of inhabiting a body to know that said body had XX chromosomes or ovaries or fallopian tubes. As the inhabitant of this body I am the sole expert on its state and status and this is not a female body. My existence and the existence of so many other people who do not fit into strict sex and/or gender binaries completely invalidates the 'wrong-body' narrative and questions whether or not there could even ever be a single perfect narrative to understand transness.

Spanish philosopher Paul B. Preciado frames a compelling 'beyond the binary' narrative in their book *Testo Junkie*. They relay a lot of experiences that will be familiar to many trans people (such as childhood gender policing and the complex feelings surrounding taking hormones), but in explaining their relationship to gender they reject both binary options presented to them, stating: 'I do not want the female gender that has been assigned to me at birth. Neither do I want the male gender that transsexual medicine can furnish and that the state will award me if I behave in the right way. I don't want any of it' (2013: 138). They are not entirely refusing a masculine gender but rather the specifically male gender that is mediated by medical bureaucracies and state-controlled technologies which are accessible only on the basis of performing appropriate masculinity. Furthermore, they describe the reason for their taking testosterone as one of disruption rather than transition:

> It's not a matter of going from woman to man, from man to woman, but of contaminating the molecular bases of the production of sexual difference, with the understanding that these two states of being, male and female, exist only as 'political fictions,' as somatic effects of the technical process of normalization. (Preciado, 2013: 142)

Here, Preciado takes on not just the gender binary but also the (related) sex binary. They identify sex as socially constructed, later elaborating: 'There are not two sexes, but a multiplicity of genetic, hormonal, chromosomal, genital, sexual, and sensual configurations. There is no empirical truth to male or female gender beyond an assemblage of normative cultural fictions' (Preciado, 2013: 263). I go into this idea in greater detail in the next chapter but this understanding of the diversity of various sexual characteristics and the way they are socially defined and redefined (or refuse to be defined) is the most valuable insight provided by the 'beyond the binary' narrative.

While this 'beyond the binary' narrative fits better with my experience and that of some other trans people, applying it too broadly would be a mistake. When eschewing the wrong-body model Bettcher highlights that this 'beyond the binary' narrative is the only alternative model of transness that is widely discussed. This model claims 'that because transgender people don't fit neatly into the two dichotomous categories of man and woman, attempts are made to force them into this binary system' and that trans people are simply people who don't fit into a binary gender system (Bettcher, 2014: 384). The 'beyond the binary' model, while not as widely accepted and therefore perhaps not as pressing to dismantle as the 'wrong-body' model, is still incomplete and overly simplistic. People of course do identify with the categories of 'man' and 'woman' (whether or not they are trans) so as an overarching model it disregards the validity of self-identification which is so crucial to trans people. This model would imply that, since trans people are supposedly outside the binary gender system, that trans woman is a different gender category than cis woman and the same for the categories of trans and cis man. Therefore, any discussion of breaking gender binaries can only be applied to people who identify as breaking those binaries and cannot be a broad sweeping central narrative. Furthermore, neither the 'wrong-body' model nor the 'beyond the binary' model offers security or certainty of validity for trans people's claims to their gender. As an alternative Bettcher offers the view that rather than opposing gender binaries (or being trapped in the wrong body), trans people challenge the perceived reality of a relationship between gender presentation and genitals. The gendered terms of 'man' and 'woman', 'male' and 'female' have multiple and flexible meanings, perhaps even an infinite number of meanings for each individual who experiences 'maleness' and 'femaleness', 'manhood' and 'womanhood'. As Judith Butler notes, this is not simply because people who break gendered norms exist but rather because stable definitions of gender do not exist:

> If one 'is' a woman, that is surely not all one is; the term fails to be exhaustive, not because a pregendered 'person' transcends the specific paraphernalia of its gender, but because gender is not always constituted coherently or consistently in different historical contexts, and because gender intersects with racial, class, ethnic, sexual, and regional modalities of discursively constituted identities. (Butler, 1990: 4)

Therefore, binary trans people are not breaking the categories of male and female but are rather redefining and expanding what those categories mean, and non-binary trans people are adding a category, or rather many categories, to the list.

3

Re-understanding sex and gender

> Recognising that sex is socially constructed is not to deny that material reality exists—simply that the meaning ascribed to biology occurs as a social process, and this has changed and continues to change over time.
>
> Vincent (2018: 45)

In this chapter I examine how people attribute sex and gender to others, which illuminates a lot about how we think about bodies and gender. Looking at some of the specific features that are often used in attribution, I question the importance or relevance of attributing sex and gender at all. Finally, I will apply this analysis to understand the role of sex and gender in healthcare.

Sex and gender attribution

The biggest issue with the idea of male-bodiedness and female-bodiedness is the question of what makes a 'biological man' or a 'biological woman' in the first place. This sex binary also does not account for intersex people so it is already invalid as a dichotomy. If we take the binary aspect out of the equation and look at male-bodied and female-bodied as merely two possible types of bodies out of many, there is still a definitional issue. No two bodies are exactly alike[1] so even with humans allegedly being sexually dimorphic, all male bodies are not alike and neither are all female bodies. This understanding challenges a simple model of human sexual dimorphism: 'Biologists and medical scientists recognize, of course, that absolute dimorphism is a Platonic ideal not actually achieved in the natural world. Nonetheless, the normative nature of medical science uses as an assumption, the proposition that for each sex there is a single, correct developmental pathway' (Blackless et al, 2000: 151).

The embracing of this impossible ideal of absolute sexual dimorphism is what provides existing definitions of these types of bodies: 'most consider that at the level of chromosomes, hormones, and genitals, dimorphism is absolute and, by implication, such traits are discrete rather than quantitative … however, developmental biology suggests that a belief in absolute sexual dimorphism is wrong' (Blackless et al, 2000: 163).

If a holistic definition of male-bodiedness and female-bodiedness is insufficient, then the body would have to be broken down into components and those components labeled as male or female. Then the question becomes how many 'male' or 'female' components does a body need to have to be labeled one way or the other? How is a body with breasts and a penis labeled? How about a body with no breasts, facial hair, a penis, a uterus, and ovaries? These hypothetical bodies need not belong to trans people but trans people certainly problematize the idea of easily categorizable male and female bodies. What makes a penis, a lack of breasts, testicles, facial hair, et cetera. male, and breasts, the lack of a penis, lack of facial hair, a uterus, vagina, ovaries, et cetera, female in the first place? If it is about perceived reproductive capabilities then is a woman only female from the start of menstruation to the beginning of menopause and a few days a month? Do we keep our gender after we die (Kessler and McKenna, 1978/2006)? Which sex characteristics are prioritized in determining gender over others? The only quality used to medically label bodies in the immediate moment after birth is the external appearance of genitalia, so that factor is definitely privileged, but is it all about genitalia? What about chromosomes? The same body using different criteria could be identified as male-bodied, female-bodied, or lying outside that binary classification.

In their 1978 article 'Toward a Theory of Gender', psychologists Suzanne Kessler and Wendy McKenna asked participants to identify whether people were male or female when given different information across two separate studies. In the first study the researchers had participants ask ten 'yes' or 'no' questions and then decide after each question whether the person they were asking about was male or female. The participants were unaware, however, that the answers to their questions were a predetermined, random 'yes' or 'no'. The answers did not correlate with any actual person and this led to many gendered 'inconsistencies'. The participants explained these away, such as rationalizing that some women are very tall and that some men have protruding breasts. Only 25 percent of people asked about the person's genitals straight away: 'when asked after the game why they did not ask about genitals, players explained that it would have been tantamount to asking "Is this person a male (or female)?", which was an unacceptable question since finding the answer was the object of the game' (Kessler and McKenna, 1978/2006: 167).

Of those who did ask about genitals, some refused to continue with the rest of the ten questions, believing that they had an unequivocal answer. From this Kessler and McKenna concluded that in gender attribution, physical and biological characteristics are more important than other social information and once someone has decided on a gender attribution they can filter all other information to fit into that. In other words, to participants, gender equaled genitals. The most ubiquitous real-life example of this is doctors proclaiming 'it's a boy' or 'it's a girl' purely based on genital appearance either after birth or even sooner in an ultrasound.

The second study Kessler and McKenna conducted used transparent overlays, each with a different physical characteristic that could be combined to create a sketch of a whole person. There were 11 overlays[2] to create 96 total possible combinations and each combination was shown to five men and five women for a total of 960 participants. Each participant was asked if the figure was male or female, how confident they were, and how they would change the figure to make it the 'other' gender. From this study they found that participants were more likely to label figures as male. 'Feminine' characteristics were ignored or seen as masculine when in combination with characteristics seen as masculine: 'the only sign of femaleness is an absence of male cues' (Kessler and McKenna, 1978/2006: 171). Genitals were the most important signifier and once gender attribution was made on the basis of genitals all other characteristics could be explained away. However, penises were more likely to result in a male identification, regardless of other characteristics, than a vulva was to result in a female identification. Participants were also most confident with their gender attribution when the image included a penis. When asked what they would change about the image to change its gender attribution, many said they would remove the penis but very few said they would add a vulva, and conversely a similar number said they would add a penis but very few said they would remove the vulva. So not only does gender equal genitals, but 'gender attribution is, for the most part, genital attribution; and genital attribution is essentially penis attribution' (Kessler and McKenna, 1978/2006: 173).

Gender attribution, they found, is not a process that happens anew with each encounter, but is rather a strong first impression:

> Almost nothing can discredit a gender attribution once it is made. Even the loss of the original criteria used to make the attribution might well become irrelevant. The man might shave his beard; the woman might have a mastectomy. The gender attribution will not change, though, merely because these signs no longer exist. (Kessler and McKenna, 1978/2006: 177)

This can make things difficult for trans people when interacting with people who knew them before they were out or who know they are trans. These binary, dichotomous, and distinct gender attributions persist despite people understanding that the reality of gender expression is far more diverse. For example, as Kessler and McKenna explain, people can conceive of a woman without breasts, and yet the presence of breasts is still most likely to result in a female gender attribution.

> Our reality is constructed in such a way that biology is seen as the ultimate truth. ... Scientific knowledge does not inform the answer to 'What makes a person either a man or a woman?' Rather it justifies (and appears to give grounds for) the already existing knowledge that a person is either a woman or a man and that there is no problem in differentiating between the two. (Kessler and McKenna, 1978/2006: 178–179)

Kessler and McKenna explain that previous models that seek to do away with gender dichotomies ignore the strength of the physical dichotomies they are derived from and rely upon. In order to truly allow for the full diversity of gendered experience I will argue that gender needs to be revealed as a social construction in all of its forms, including the physical.

Sex and gender attribution in healthcare

The gender attribution paradigm explained here can be seen in a variety of ways when trans people interact with a cisnormative[3] healthcare system. Ben, a transmasculine person, told me about his experience getting his Pre-T blood test[4] results:

> 'It was really funny actually. ... I went to get the test done, I did actually manage to get the bloods out of me and into the system whatever it is but after that point the people just got really really confused. They were just like "Uh, I don't know what to do." ... I called them to ask for my results and because my voice wasn't, I sound like a female basically, they just were so confused and they asked me all sorts of really bizarre questions. They asked me ... if I had erectile dysfunction because something to do with the testosterone levels. ... I was like "No, I just need my blood results" and they ... they were really confused and they were, I think they thought I was a cis male with some kind of hormonal problem and also erectile dysfunction ... who needed their bloods tested and then when they gave me the results they told me that I should come in straight away because I was very low on testosterone.' (Ben)

The medical professionals in this interaction were assuming Ben was cis. When they were confused by his high-pitched voice they assumed he was a cis woman and when they thought his low testosterone was concerning and potentially causing erectile dysfunction they assumed he was a cis man. Despite the fact that, barring a hormonal issue, all humans produce testosterone, they assumed someone getting their testosterone levels tested had to be male, and they further assumed that as a male he would have a penis, that that penis would and should be capable of an erection, and that he should have testosterone levels within a certain range. This series of assumptions, all based in cisnormativity, shows a lack of education and/or understanding on the part of these medical professionals in regards to the trans patients they are treating. This is not an isolated occurrence as another participant, Adam, was even advised during his gender identity clinic (GIC) appointment to make certain that he reiterated to the people taking his bloods that they needed to check testosterone levels because many of the clinic's other patients had had an issue with the people testing the bloods seeing an 'f' marker in the system and ignoring the request to test testosterone levels, perhaps assuming it to be a mistake. Assumptions around gendered bodies are so strong that rather than running all of the tests requested on the form as is standard practice, and testing testosterone levels even if it was a mistake on the form and would do no harm, lab technicians decide not to test the testosterone levels of someone they assume is female.

In the same way that gendered stereotypes obscure scientific knowledge when discussing gametes, as discussed in Emily Martin's work in the previous chapter, these sociocultural assumptions block healthcare providers from giving the best care to their trans patients. Instead of traditional gender roles the stereotypes they are relying on are false certainties such as 'all men have penises', 'women don't need their testosterone levels tested', and even 'an "f" marker in their file means the patient is a woman'. Hopefully this critique will shine a light on the problematic nature of these ingrained assumptions around the relationship between gender and bodies in healthcare just as Martin did in the realm of science writing. The situations described here would not have been possible if the healthcare providers were not operating inside a powerful cisnormative paradigm. If these providers could imagine that their patients might be trans, then they would have no reason to question someone with an 'f' marker on their records getting their testosterone levels tested. This clearly shows a disconnect between what is expected of gendered bodies and the reality of bodies, a formidable barrier that trans people face while seeking healthcare and in their everyday lives.

Biological essentialism

Some anti-trans rhetoric relies heavily on the idea that there are certain biological truths that cannot be altered, that the reality of being born in a male or female body is absolute. The issue with this approach to labeling sex is biological essentialism. 'Instead of taking responsibility for who counts socially as a man or woman, people turn to science, trying to use the biological criteria for male to define a man and the biological criteria for female to define a woman' (Roughgarden, 2004/2013: 148). Even scholars who tout the importance of bodies in the gender discussion allow for a level of fluidity and social constructedness. Australian philosopher Elizabeth Grosz, for example, recognizes that culture inscribes our bodies 'permanently and impermeably' in specifically gendered ways (1994: 141). As a feminist scholar Grosz continually challenges the 'naturalness' attributed to bodies: '[t]here is no "natural" norm; there are only cultural forms of body, which do or do not conform to social norms' (1994: 143). Biological essentialism, on the other hand, refuses to engage in a nuanced definitional process and instead resorts to biology to define femininity and masculinity. As Judith Butler says, 'the return to Biology as the ground of a specific feminine sexuality or meaning seems to defeat the feminist premise that biology is not destiny' (1990: 41). This essentialism is not theoretically rigorous and ultimately is anti-feminist in the way it insists on linking and limiting 'womanhood' (and it is mostly womanhood as trans women are the overwhelming target of this rhetoric) to one specific biological destiny.

Attributing sex

Sex, nearly always cast as the ever constant variable in this saga of gender diversity, is in reality quite diverse in and of itself. As already explained, intersex people are people with ambiguous or a mixture of sexual characteristics, people who are not explicitly male-bodied or female-bodied. To return to and expand upon the question posed in the previous section, what makes a male body, a female body, or a non-binary body, there must be a set of criteria that defines different sexes or different types of bodies, and for these classifications to exist and then to be imposed upon people definitional criteria must be clear and in the case of multiple criteria there must be a classification hierarchy. For example, if two of the criteria for a male body would be the presence of a penis and the absence of breasts, one of these two criteria would need to be valued higher than the other to account for bodies where these two states do not exist in tandem. Currently, genitals are favored in this hierarchy: 'in order to say that a transsexual (after genital reconstruction surgery) has undergone a "sex change," we must discount other features, including chromosomes, and select genitalia as definitive' (Bettcher, 2014: 386). Preciado discusses enjoying the openness of genital possibilities that exists prior to revealing, and thus committing to, a singular genital appearance within a sexual encounter:

> I take turns imagining myself with and without a cock, and the two images keep following each other like a game on a seesaw. But I know that the moment I get undressed, she'll see only one of these bodies. Being reduced to one fixed image frightens me. I keep my clothes on a few minutes more, so I can enjoy the double option little longer. (Preciado, 2013: 88)

Similarly, Adam recalls the differing experiences of his genitals being hidden versus being visible/known in these two stories from his childhood:

> 'And so if I was being very headstrong that day and going "No, I wanna wear the boy's bathing suit, I wanna wear this bathing suit" … cause I don't think I ever called it the boy's bathing suit I was just like "This is the one I wanna wear", she just didn't argue she was like "Yeah whatever" and then I'd sort of go running around this wading pool with like just shorts on and you know everybody assumed I was just a boy with long hair because from, you know, hiding the sort of area of genitals there was no hugely defining difference. And I should point out that when my brother was born there was like a moment where my mom had us both in the bath and I said, you know, "When, when's my penis gonna grow?" and she said "No … it's not gonna happen", and I, I was probably four and … I sort of went "Okay", but inside my brain I was like "Oh you'll see", like this four-year-old thinking she's wrong.' (Adam)

In Adam's experience his genitals were the only thing that may have prevented him from passing as a boy as a child and they are something he remembers wanting to change from a very young age.

Genitals are clearly a key player in labeling bodies but there is a lot of diversity to be found where they are concerned. With genitals, as with other characteristics it is not obvious what the 'rule' is because, as American evolutionary biologist Joan Roughgarden notes, 'when it comes to humans, the biological criteria for male and female don't coincide 100 percent with present-day social criteria for man and woman' (2004/2013: 148). Even though Adam desires to one day have metoidioplasty[5] which will give him a penis by many if not all definitions, is he not still currently male and does this male identity apply to his body as well? At what point does his or anyone else's body become a male body? If it is when they obtain a penis, what defines a penis? Is it only a clitoris that has diverged developmentally to form a penis in utero, meaning trans men never have male bodies? Is it the result of any genital surgery? Is the very different result of metoidioplasty as opposed to phalloplasty to be counted? Is it the enlarged clitoris (or what is often called a clitoris[6]) resultant from testosterone therapy? If not, then why is a clitoris that develops into a penis in utero valued over a clitoris that develops into a penis later in life through hormone therapy and/or surgery? Or is a penis merely whatever the possessor of the penis decides it to be?

While important, genitals are not typically used in gendering bodies in interpersonal interactions on a day to day basis, simply because they are not often visible. That is where secondary sex characteristics, all sexually dimorphic features that are not part of the reproductive system, move to the forefront. As Preciado notes, 'the beard and the voice, and not the penis and the vagina or X and Y chromosomes, are the dominant cultural public signifiers of gender in our society' (2013: 227). Speaking voice is particularly interesting as it is not a visible feature, but 'male bodies' are still supposed to produce a low-pitched voice and 'female bodies' a high-pitched voice, related to the size of the voice box and the length of the vocal chords which are understood to be sexually dimorphic characteristics. Even for cis people there is a massive range of what 'high pitched' and 'low pitched' can mean as well as overlaps in the center where cis men with higher voices and cis women with lower voices may reach the same pitch or even pass each other toward the other side of the vocal spectrum. However, a trans person may still be outed by their speaking voice being inconsistent with what people are expecting to hear, so this inexact criteria is a point of concern. I avoid speaking to strangers as much as possible, particularly when accessing a gendered space like the men's bathroom. Adam talked about "constantly worrying … wondering if the shopkeeper is gonna think my voice is low enough for a man or if he's gonna misgender me". This is concerning because if trans people like Adam are 'constantly worrying' about being misgendered in public they may withdraw somewhat from public life. That kind of social isolation leads to poor health and mental health outcomes (see Trout, 1980; Cacioppo and Hawkley, 2003; Tomaka et al, 2006; Hall-Lande et al, 2007; Cacioppo and Hawkley, 2009; Cornwell and Waite, 2009).

In addition to being socially isolating, being misgendered can have a dissociating effect. When I know someone is talking about me from social or context clues but they use female pronouns or terminology it feels as though they are talking about someone else and that dissonance is distressing. Another participant, Ben, said: "The worst part is when if they gender you correctly and then you open your mouth and you speak and then they apologize." I too have experienced the frustrating exchange of being called 'sir' only for the person to profusely apologize and call me 'ma'am' once they hear my voice. Some trans people go through voice training to learn to raise or lower their pitch and there are surgical options available to adjust the size of the voice box and length of the vocal chords to achieve a more 'masculine' or 'feminine' voice. Still others come up with their own solutions to this problem, like Ben: "When I was pre-testosterone, I'm partially deaf but I'm not fully deaf … so I have like a lot of deaf friends and everything so I would often pretend I was fully deaf so that I wouldn't have to use my voice so that I could pass easier." Ben was able to use sign language to avoid being outed by his higher pitched voice, an eminently creative adaptation. Although cis men have vocal pitches within a wide range, Ben was worried that his higher pitched voice would out him. In this instance his voice (over physical characteristics) was something he could control by opting to not speak so he did so in order to pass, the same way people will use clothing, makeup, hair style, and so on. Genitals and voice are just two examples but any characteristic that is supposed to be able to identify the sex of a human body is going to be complicated by (and complicate the lives of) trans people.

The disconnect between biological and cultural definitions is the cause of much confusion and debate. When biologists are sexing bodies, or any organism, it comes back to the sperm and the egg. It is important to note that I am merely relaying one discourse around sex that is used in biology here. As I will go on to explain, I am not endorsing this discourse nor its application to human bodies. To do so would be tantamount to biological essentialism, which as I discussed earlier must be resisted. In this biological discourse, a male of a species makes small gametes (called sperm) and a female of a species makes large gametes (called eggs). However, there is still allowance for an exciting amount of diversity within this classification system. There are instances in different species of animals and plants of females changing to males, males changing to females, changing back and forth between male and female, and the states of maleness and femaleness existing concurrently. 'These examples of sequential, simultaneous, and crisscrossing hermaphrodism show that male and female functions don't need to be packaged into lifelong distinct bodies' (Roughgarden, 2004/2013: 154). Furthermore, sex itself refers to the mode of reproduction which humans and many other species employ which involves two parties and the mixing of genes. With this in mind it makes sense that sex classification is based on gamete size, but then is there any usefulness in using sex as a classification system at all beyond discussions of reproduction? As Roughgarden notes, it is extremely limited in what it tells us and is insufficient to describe humans and our vast and diverse social classifications. While I feel I would be remiss in not addressing human biological diversity it is not the existence of such diversity that validates trans identity. Just as biological essentialism and presuming binary sex is a poor way of modeling gender, so too is any model that relies on a definitive, causal relationship between biology and gender. I merely hope to point out that it is not only the binary gender model that is incorrect but also the binary sex model, and that the two models are linked.

Postgenderism

One approach to the dismantling of sex and gender binaries is postgenderism, or a movement toward the elimination of gender through social change and advances in biotechnology. Inspiration can be drawn from societies that have already broken the gender binary or have perhaps never had it, however a truly postgender society would be a completely new phenomena. The existence of trans people, which inherently challenges binary gender and sex categories, can be used as an example of a movement toward postgenderism:

> [T]oday's transgender movement is a roiling, radical critique of the limits of gender roles, with folks living in totally new categories, such as non-op transsexual, TG butch, femme queen, cross-dresser, third gender, drag king or queen and transboi. These genderqueer activists and theorists advocate postgender attitudes, such as promoting the use of gender-neutral pronouns such as 'ze', 'per', and 'zir'. (Dvorsky and Hughes, 2008: 7)

For many of these people who don't fit into the gender binary simply living as themselves is a revolutionary act. However, 'while transgendered bodies can call our categories of sex and gender into question, they can also confirm and reinforce the conventional gender system in the way that transgendered bodies are judged and evaluated for sex reassignment surgery' which is distinctly not postgenderist (Johnson and Repta, 2012: 33). Some trans people are very comfortable within binary gender categories and others may portray that they are in order to access transition related healthcare.

While many trans people do fit into the categories of 'woman' and 'man' (although many also do not), it is the concept of transness that supports many of these postgenderist ideas. Those who do fit into that mold may feel social pressure to conform to a certain gender presentation to access healthcare, to feel secure, and so on, or they may simply feel most comfortable in a traditionally masculine or feminine gender expression. Within medical spaces, trans people often feel they have to alter, slightly or drastically, the ways in which they present themselves in the context of the GIC in order to be approved for the hormones and/or surgery they are seeking. As Dean Spade notes in their piece 'Mutilating Gender':

> The self-determination of trans people in crafting our gender expression is compromised by the rigidity of the diagnostic and treatment criteria. ... To adopt the medical understanding of transsexuality is to agree that [Sex Reassignment Surgery] is the unfortunate treatment of an unfortunate condition, to accept that gender norm adherence is fortunate and healthy, and to undermine the threat to a dichotomous gender system which trans experience can pose. The reification of the violence of compulsory gender norm adherence, and the submission of trans bodies to a norm-producing medical discipline, is too high a price for a small hope of conditional tolerance. (Spade, 2000/2006: 329)

This harmful phenomenon of gender norm adherence that Spade describes conceals layers of identity and diversity. For example, Ben identifies as transmasculine and has said he is more male than not but "if there's some other option I usually tick that unless I feel like the place that I'm you know at is gonna discriminate against me and then I will always tick 'M', or 'F' depending on where I am". The finer details of his identity are being erased in these instances. This becomes especially relevant when, as Johnson and Repta note, trans bodies are being evaluated for transition related healthcare. Here Ben describes his experience of obtaining his prescription for testosterone and feeling like he had to tailor his story to what they wanted to hear:

> 'The vibe was the kind of thing it was expected I think, although it wasn't really expressly said so … I just kind of gauged what they were doing and it seemed like when I was being assessed that's what they were looking for just ticking boxes, I think he was literally ticking boxes as I was going … cause I didn't go in there thinking I'm gonna lie through my teeth like I kind of just got in there and I thought "Ugh this environment is a little bit like intimidating I'm just gonna see how it goes".' (Ben)

Ben's experience shows how trans people being categorized by the healthcare system under traditionally gendered labels may largely be a case of confirmation bias, a self-fulfilling prophecy. To access hormones and certain surgeries, trans people ensure that they are ticking the proper boxes, such as expressing interest in a 'complete' transition and monitoring their gender presentation when attending GIC appointments to come across as suitably masculine or feminine.[7] This in turn validates the boxes and makes it appear as though this ordered view of gender is accurate. In reality, many people do not fit into these discrete categories. This would include all non-binary people including non-binary men and non-binary women as well as people who may identify their gender within the binary but break the norms associated with that gender in some way, such as a femme trans man. Not being able to tick those boxes authentically and showing the invalidity of constructed gender categories could be seen to support postgenderism.

The trouble here comes with radicalizing trans bodies, as Bettcher points to in her critique of the 'beyond the binary model'. Just as the medicalization of transness pathologizes trans people, so postgenderism politicizes them. An understanding of transness as something that is automatically radical and political is limiting and many trans people do not understand themselves that way. Adam demonstrated this when he explained how he just sees himself as a regular guy:

> '[I]t's just an easier way to help them sort of understand … if they, they wanna ask some questions I just say oh yeah I'm transgender, man, transgender male, but personally I just identify as a man cause I just I feel like you know there are ways in which I've never been great with labels, and trans is not something that I necessarily asked to be and that's, I'm not saying there's anything wrong with it, but just my

own like personal gut feeling is that it's another label that you know society has said well this is something you are to point you out as being different from the regular thing, the normal thing, and I don't really see that much difference between me and cis guys.' (Adam)

Here Adam is rejecting the idea that there is anything inherently radical or even different about him. This sentiment was also echoed by another participant, Dan. To them, adding the qualifier of 'transgender' separates them from other men and makes them feel other. Particularly because of the violence and harassment faced by trans people, normalizing sex and gender diversity is as crucial as ever (Factor and Rothblum, 2007; Greenberg, 2012; Testa et al, 2012; Lee and Kwan, 2014). This does not mean doing away with the concept of gender altogether as proposed by postgenderists, but simply broadening the understanding of what gender is and can be, responding to an oppressive system not by rejecting it but by embracing, reclaiming, and reshaping it.

The reintegration of sex and gender

As an alternative to postgenderism, I will propose a reintegration of sex and gender in our understanding of trans identity. The initial distinction between the two terms came as a response to 'sex' and 'gender' incorrectly being used interchangeably. In 'Disaggregating Gender from Sex and Sexual Orientation: The Effeminate Man in the Law and Feminist Jurisprudence', legal scholar Mary Anne C. Case argues passionately and thoroughly for a separation of the understandings of sex, gender, and sexual orientation. In this case it is in the context of US law but many of the arguments presented have broader reaching applications. One of the multitude of examples cited as a reason to separate sex from gender is a situation where men were barred from serving on a jury in a paternity case. In this instance, Justice Scalia argued, and Case agrees, that there was no gender[8] discrimination because feminine and masculine men were excluded equally but that there was sex discrimination (Case, 1995: 11). Case further explains that this separation is crucial for protecting things like Title IX[9] because as gender (expression) becomes more fluid the law must be able to distinguish to be able to protect, for example, masculine women from discrimination. Overall, Case concludes as follows:

> In arguing that the treatment of the exceptional effeminate man teaches us much about that of both feminine and masculine women as well as masculine men, I hope to have shown how, once again, the margins can illuminate the center; and to have taken steps to make the world safe for us all, norms and exceptions, men and women, masculine and feminine,

and every shade in between. By disaggregating gender from sex and sexual orientation focusing attention on the reasons why the feminine might have been devalued in both women and men, I hope to protect what is valuable about the traditionally feminine without essentializing it, limiting it to women, or limiting women to it. (Case, 1995: 105)

These aims are admirable and aspirational and were another necessary step toward fully understanding what gender is and the role it plays in society, however I argue that this need not be the final step.

The brief yet important separation of these two concepts has provided a key understanding that sex does not determine gender and that gender is self-identified. With that understanding these two aspects of identity can again be understood in tandem, and the separation of sex and gender has served its purpose. For example, one of the key areas of focus in Case's article was employment discrimination. In this instance the first step was to show that certain 'masculine' or 'feminine' traits that made someone good for a certain job actually need not belong to men or women respectively because sex and gender are separate concepts. With that understanding, however, I argue that the next step is to show that gender identity informs sex and sex can be part of that gender expression. I argue that sex identity is just as self-identified as gender, that a person has the type of body they say they have regardless of individual features. Any type of chest is masculine if the inhabitant of that body identifies as having a masculine body. What would usually be called a penis is feminine if the inhabitant of that body identifies as having a feminine body. The sex of a body with any given combination of physical features cannot be identified by a third party observer the same way gender cannot be. This is not such a radical concept, it is a level of human diversity that is already prevalent in intersex people who are born into bodies that fall outside the sex binary, trans people who have sought transition related hormone therapy and surgeries, and in cis people who have had their bodies altered for other reasons, such as a cis woman who has had a double mastectomy as a result of breast cancer. This perspective of sex self-identification and a link between gender identity and sex identity or gender identity and sex expression would allow for more sex diversity within the norm, specifically normalizing intersex and trans bodies.

Intra-acting gender

In 'Posthumanist Performativity: Toward an Understanding of How Matter Comes to Matter', American feminist scholar Karen Barad discusses a theory of agential realism which challenges and expands upon previous models of materiality, addressing both how we understand matter epistemologically as well as how it is actually formed and altered ontologically. They also take the concept of performativity and elaborate and expand it to non-human bodies:

> How might we understand not only how human bodily contours are constituted through psychic processes but how even the very atoms that make up the biological body come to matter and, more generally, how matter makes itself felt? It is difficult to imagine how psychic and socio-historical forces alone could account for the production of matter. Surely it is the case—even when the focus is restricted to the materiality of 'human' bodies—that there are 'natural,' not merely 'social,' forces that matter. Indeed, there is a host of material-discursive forces—including ones that get labeled 'social,' 'cultural,' 'psychic,' 'economic,' 'natural,' 'physical,' 'biological,' 'geopolitical,' and 'geological'—that may be important to particular (entangled) processes of materialization. If we follow disciplinary habits of tracing disciplinary-defined causes through to the corresponding disciplinary-defined effects, we will miss all the crucial intra-actions among these forces that fly in the face of any specific set of disciplinary concerns. (Barad, 2003: 810)

This concept of intra-action directly opposes the term interaction. In an interaction there is an event between two pre-existing entities, the actors in the interaction exist and have an identity outside of the interaction itself. However intra-action asserts that the entity is itself the result of the event. The actors do not exist before or independent of the action. If you look at the gendered body through this lens there is no inherent, no innate physicality preordained by so-called biological realities. Each gendered body is the product of a unique set of intra-actions. There is no before and after, the process of discovering one's gender reflects on one's body in the past, present and future. For example, a trans man coming to understand himself as a man also develops an understanding of what his male body is in his present (whether that is a body altered through hormones and/or surgeries or not), but that can also reflect back with him re-understanding his past as having always embodied maleness even if he didn't realize it at the time and further projects into his imagining of his male future. Then if upon more realization he learns that perhaps he is a non-binary man, this too develops, reflects, and projects his understanding of himself as he continues to enact his gender, 'matter is not a fixed essence; rather, matter is substance in its intra-active becoming—not a thing but a doing, a congealing of agency' (Barad, 2003: 828). One of the ways he may enact this is through choosing a masculine name, using he/him pronouns, and generally using masculine language to refer to himself in the present and future but perhaps also in the past tense. He can ask others in his life to follow suit, which will spawn a multitude of events where intra-action can take place. While not using this specific framework, geographer Tom Delph-Janiurek states in 'Sex, Talk and Making Bodies in the Science Lab' that 'rather than simply being used to name or refer to gendered bodies, gendered forenames, pronoual referents and terms of address can be regarded as citational hailings that actually work to (re)produce gendered bodies in everyday interactions' (2001: 40). These everyday interactions are the points where intra-action takes place, constantly (re)constructing the gendered body either in accordance with or against the gendered narrative of the individual.

This ongoing body project does not only intra-act with extra-corporeal entities but can incorporate them into the corporeal. In *Volatile Bodies: Toward a Corporeal Feminism*, Elizabeth Grosz posits:

> The body image is not an isolated image of the body but necessarily involves the relations between the body, the surrounding space, other objects and bodies, and the coordinates or axes of vertical and horizontal. The body image is the condition of the subject's access to spatiality (including the spatiality of the built environment). (Grosz, 1994: 85)

If we focus on the body image being reliant in part on the body's relationship with other objects, then can those 'objects' not become part of that body? I argue that it is not just the body image that is changed here but, in some cases, the body itself. When I previously discussed different types of penises I failed to mention a penis that to others may be understood as a packer,[10] a strap-on,[11] et cetera, which has been incorporated into the corporeal identity of the individual. It may be a removable, interchangeable penis but it is a penis nonetheless. Therefore, a body without a penis is transformed into a body with a penis, even if only temporarily. Breast forms can be similarly incorporated. In these cases, the close identification with these objects change the body through these additions and/or extensions. The body is now one with a penis, breasts, and so on. We can also understand disincorpor(eal)ating practices, such as tucking[12] and binding,[13] which remove something from the corporeal identity. This removal may not even require performing an action on the body but can happen entirely through narrative means. If the methods for (re)constructing bodies are opened up beyond the limited possibilities provided by medical interventions the corporeal possibilities are endless.

The physical characteristics, however, the marks of 'nature' that lead to a baby being assigned a sex at birth, are not irrelevant because it is that act of assigning sex at birth that starts the chain of events of a gendered upbringing that results in transness existing in the first place. In 'Putting the Body's Feet on the Ground: Towards a Sociological Reconceptualization of Gendered and Sexual Embodiment', gender scholars Stevi Jackson and Sue Scott suggest that:

> [T]he gendered body is not always a sexual body, that the body can be sexual as both object and subject and that the connections between the gendered body and the sexual body require further exploration – we cannot reduce one to the other, but need to explore the relationship between them. (Jackson and Scott, 2001: 16)

Gender does not supersede sex but neither can gender be subsumed under sex. What is important is unpacking and challenging the reality of those characteristics and the meanings attached to them as well as bringing to light hidden diversity. Barad says that 'nature is neither a passive surface awaiting the mark of culture nor the end product of cultural performances' (2003: 827). All of these forces are constantly intra-acting with each other in order to create material realities.

The importance of sex self-identification

But surely sex self-identification devalues trans people who want to 'fully transition', those who seek to alter their physical body in order to completely align it with what is traditionally defined as a female body or a male body. If, for example, a trans woman was born in a female body, simply a different type of female body, and if she is therefore not 'trapped' in a male body, then why should she ever want hormone therapy and surgeries? And if that is the case then why should the National Health Service provide these things to trans people? I argue that sex self-identification is crucial to good health and is therefore a right that everyone should have access to regardless of gender identity or experience. Opening up possibilities for sexed embodiment beyond strict, binary definitions does specifically uplift non-op trans people, people who seek a 'partial'[14] and/or non-linear transition, intersex, and non-binary people. However, binary-oriented trans people and/or people who seek a 'complete', linear transition also benefit from this perspective. If sex is self-identified in the sense that the inhabitant of a body has definitional power over that body, then it also stands to reason that sex is self-identified in the sense that the inhabitant of that body can also define what their body should look like and what features it should and shouldn't have. American sociologist James Hughes calls this 'morphological self-determination':

> As the medical model of gender dysphoria is challenged by morphological liberationism on the one hand, and bioconservativism on the other, it will be difficult to make the case for covering the therapies with public or private insurance. But instead of reifying the

medical model, transgender therapy should be used to challenge the illusory therapy/enhancement distinction, and establish that facilitating full self-expression is as legitimate a use of biotechnology as the fixing of diseases and disorders. There is little difference in the utility produced in someone's life from plastic surgery after an accident or burn, and plastic surgery to adjust a feature that has caused life-long dissatisfaction. There is no reason for insurance to discriminate against the latter in favor of the former. Why is breast reconstruction for the woman recovering from breast cancer surgery politically privileged over breast construction for the trans-woman? Neither are 'medically necessary' and both done to give psychological relief. ... Transgendered individuals are entitled to access to medical technology not because, as the advocates of the medical model such as Dr. Spack assert, they have a medical condition that demands correction, but because we should respect the right to morphological self-determination. (Hughes, 2006: 11)

It is crucial that these two tenets, sex self-identification and a right to morphological self-determination, go hand in hand. This makes the most sense for a model that would try to understand the experiences of an incredibly diverse group of people as well as allow them access to life-saving services. And they are life-saving: trans people are far more likely to attempt suicide[15] than the general population and are at a greater risk for physical violence, drug and alcohol abuse, smoking, and other risk factors that negatively impact health (Grant et al, 2010). These increased risk factors are in addition to increased difficulty accessing healthcare, particularly mental healthcare. One participant, Adam, was experiencing severe depression and anxiety[16] and initially had difficulty getting a referral for mental health services because he was already in the queue for a GIC and he was told that the psychologists at the clinic would help him. Once he convinced his healthcare providers that his mental health needs were beyond the scope of the gender clinic he ended up being referred for crisis mental health services through his London borough, but when he called to schedule the appointment he was consistently misgendered over the phone despite correcting the receptionist every time. This was extremely upsetting to him, particularly in his already fragile mental state. This exact lack of training on how to deal with trans patients puts yet another barrier between trans people and good physical and mental health. This is important and this theory is not stating that sex doesn't matter or treating the subject lightly in any way. It rather aims toward a model of sex and gender that fits with the reality of diverse bodies and respects an inhabitant of a body's own experience of being in that body, whether or not they see that body as currently incongruous with their gender identity.

The challenge with this reintegration perspective is that it is itself a challenge. It is a provocation to accepted norms surrounding sex and gender as well as to the dominant narratives as they are employed for greater trans acceptance. Difficult as it may be, however, this perspective is more accurate in terms of the real life experiences of trans people and more inclusive than the 'wrong-body' narrative, the 'beyond the binary' narrative, or indeed then postgenderism. The theory allows for the inclusion of non-binary sex and gender identities, it centers the subject as the preeminent expert on their own body and self, and it celebrates rather than erases diverse human experiences of sex and gender. Chase Strangio puts it beautifully when they say:

> I was assigned female at birth, but I have never had a female body. If it takes longer to convince the world of that than it would to simply say that I was born with a female body but am now male, I am invested in that longer path, because ultimately we will all be better off when we can challenge the idea that our body parts define us. (Strangio, 2016)

4

Medicalization

> 'My experience with gender and with chronic illness are quite, they parallel each other quite a lot I think.'
>
> Carey

In this chapter I highlight a formidable barrier to trans health: the medicalization of transness under healthcare systems, including the NHS, as 'gender identity disorder'. The problem with medicalization is two-fold. Firstly, it stigmatizes transness which is a barrier to good mental health and, secondly, it creates medical gatekeepers and bureaucratic barriers[1] that delay or prevent trans people from accessing quality healthcare. To fully understand this problem I map transness using medical sociologist Peter Conrad's framework of medicalization, expanding upon it throughout in order to unpack the ways medical social control is enacted on trans people. I conclude with an argument for demedicalization, looking at how trans services would manifest if they were not treating a medical condition but rather were providing access to necessary medical technologies.

What is medicalization?

To understand medicalization I am focusing on two works by Peter Conrad. Firstly, I will be using 'Medicalization and Social Control' (1992), because it contains a thorough analysis of the relevant (particularly post-1980) literature on medicalization. Secondly, I will be pulling from 'The Shifting Engines of Medicalization' (2005) which provides a more contemporary update to that previous work. While Conrad only mentions transness briefly, I am using these theories to understand on a micro level the way that transness specifically is medicalized. In 'Medicalization and Social Control', Conrad explains that '"medicalization" describes a process by which non-medical problems become defined and treated as medical problems, usually in terms of illness and disorders' (1992: 209). Conditions can be medicalized to a greater or lesser degree and it is a complex process with care providers, researchers, government bodies, patients, and other agents all playing a part. It is a broader social pattern that can be deliberate or unintentional on the part of the medical profession. It is also often a gendered phenomenon, as 'gender segmentation is a propitious strategy for defining problems and promoting medical solutions, both exploiting and reinforcing gender boundaries', something that becomes especially relevant for trans people (Conrad, 2005: 11). Specifically, Conrad identifies three types of medicalization: conceptual medicalization, institutional medicalization, and interactional medicalization; further differentiating between 'deviant' medicalized behaviors and medicalized behaviors that are part of a natural life course. As for what causes medicalization, Conrad highlights secularization and the nature of the medical profession itself as two possible culprits. Finally, Conrad delves into the effects of medicalization as a form of social control and the resulting push-back for demedicalization in some cases, all of which can be understood through and applied to the lens of trans studies.

Conceptual medicalization

Conceptual medicalization deals with language and the ways in which problems are defined and discussed. One example is the gradual cultural shift from describing people struggling with addiction as wayward people who have made bad choices to understanding them as sick people struggling with the disease of addiction (Schneider, 1978). This does not require any direct action on the part of the medical profession and is a social rather than a medical realization, although the medical profession may later cosign the medicalization, as is the case in this example where medicine has legitimized the diagnosis of addiction as a disease that can be treated. Conceptual medicalization does not necessarily refer to treatment explicitly but rather reframes the 'problem' itself. It takes a societal phenomenon and transforms it into a medical disease or disorder with the use of certain types of language. The phenomena is described as an 'illness', definitional power is taken from the individual and given to medical professionals to 'diagnose' the 'illness', experiences and behaviors become 'symptoms', and certain associated actions are deemed 'treatments'.

In the case of transness,[2] the 'illness' is gender identity disorder (or any of the many names by which it goes), which doctors legitimize with a diagnosis using symptomatic criteria such as the experience of 'gender dysphoria', while actions taken by trans people such as Hormone Replacement Therapy (HRT) and certain surgeries are the 'treatments'. Conceptual medicalization can clearly be seen here in the historical 'shift' from transness being culturally viewed as a perverse choice and even a criminal offense[3] to a mental illness which has then been cosigned by the psychological profession with the ever evolving diagnosis of different gender identity disorders. The shift is an incomplete one, however, as the state still maintains some control, particularly over the process of having one's gender legally changed, a process they collaborate with medical practitioners to gatekeep, as I discuss in more detail in what follows. Particularly in the UK, where there is a nationalized healthcare system, state and medical social control are complexly intertwined (Harrison and Ahmad, 2000; Abraham, 2009).

Institutional medicalization

Institutional medicalization takes place within organizations such as schools, prisons, charities, and various government agencies. A classic example of institutional medicalization would be schools labeling rambunctious children as 'hyperactive' in order to offer them certain accommodations. Even with this form of medicalization, as with the school example, the organization may consult medical professionals but it does not require their direct action. In this case, 'physicians may function as gatekeepers for benefits that are only legitimate in organizations that adopt a medical definition and approach to a problem, but where the everyday routine work is accomplished by nonmedical personnel' (Conrad, 1992: 211). So, while children may require a formal diagnosis to receive services, the actual work of medicalizing these students and separating them from their peers is done by non-medical personnel within the school system (Phillips, 2006).

With trans people, this type of medicalization can be seen in the UK's government bureaucracy. Many trans people want their birth certificate and other identifying documents to reflect their correct gender rather than the one they were assigned at birth. To do this in the UK you need to acquire a Gender Recognition Certificate (GRC), wherein you prove to the government that you are indeed the gender you say you are according to their criteria. It is of the utmost importance to note that currently only binary genders are accepted so non-binary trans people are completely excluded from obtaining any legal recognition. If you would like to change your gender to either male or female, then a doctor's statement confirming a diagnosis of gender dysphoria is required. In the application form medical authority is valued over the authority of the trans person. After all of the usual biographic information and a section in which you state the date you started living as your gender (as if that is a clear or reasonable question to ask anyone), there is the required medical report from a practitioner specializing in gender dysphoria then the medical report from a second practitioner not necessarily specializing in gender dysphoria. Only after those does the statutory declaration come, where the applicant legally swears that they are the gender they say they are. It is also important to note that if they are married or in a civil partnership, there is an additional section where their spouse has to sign off, further chipping away at trans people's autonomy (Government Digital Service, 2014).[4] From the fact that this process exists at all to how it is constructed and carried out promotes a medicalized model of transness that is nevertheless not carried out solely by medical professionals.

Interactional medicalization

The third and final form of medicalization profiled by Conrad is interactional medicalization, which is medicalization that takes place within the doctor–patient relationship. When someone goes to a medical professional with a problem and that professional claims ownership of that problem and says on a very basic level, 'this is what is wrong with you' (diagnosis) and 'this is what we [the medical profession] are going to do to fix it' (treatment), interactional medicalization is taking place. This is where the medical profession is undoubtedly directly involved in the process of medicalization, although it does not need to be intentional on the part of the individual medical professional. Rather, interactional medicalization is embedded in the medical system as a whole. When it is unintentional the medical professionals are simply following their own training, although their actions can also be informed by their own personal feelings and ideologies. It is, however, the most visible and obvious form of medicalization, particularly to the people experiencing it.

With trans people this happens when they seek transition related healthcare from medical professionals. Because many trans people seek things like HRT therapy and different surgeries which have been wholly claimed by the medical sphere, they must go through the medical system to access them. This is where many trans people can most readily see the impact that the medicalization of their bodies and identities has on their lives as they encounter a medical system that claims them and yet is ill-equipped to actually help them (House of Commons Women and Equalities Committee, 2016). Interactional medicalization can be seen when trans people go to their General Practitioners (GPs) for help and are referred to a gender clinic to be diagnosed with 'gender dysphoria' and put on a linear transition path which they see as the treatment for this 'disease'. That linear transition starts with a social transition to gain 'real life experience'.[5] A social transition consists of the trans person coming out to their friends, family, and other people in their life as trans. From there it may include changing their name and gender markers on identification, adopting the clothing and hairstyles associated with their gender, using pronouns associated with their gender, and so on. Real life experience is the term the NHS uses to refer to these steps. The people looking for hormones and/or surgery will at some stage ask their GP for a referral to a gender clinic.[6] Transmasculine people are then expected to wait for 'top surgery' (double mastectomy).[7] The final step is entering the queue for various 'bottom surgeries' of which there are many possibilities. It is relevant to note here that adhering to or deviating from this pathway does not say anything about the person who is embarking on that path, as trans health scholar Ben Vincent notes in their 2018 book *Transgender Health: A Practitioner's Guide to Binary and Non-Binary Trans Patient Care*:

> It is important that clinicians do not assume that binary-oriented trans people have one discrete set of needs while non-binary trans people have another. Patients should be considered in an individual manner, such that a binary-oriented trans person might want a less typical transition pathway or a non-binary person might want a very traditional transition, without this undermining the reality of their experience of gender. (Vincent, 2018: 165–166)

What is described here is an extremely simplified outline of the current pathway but it represents the way the medical system situates trans people and understands the process of transitioning, as completely binary and linear.

There is another concerning layer to do with the medicalization of transness, which is that some medical professionals do not recognize transness (Grant et al, 2010). Due to gaps in their training, personal feelings such as religious or political ideologies, or other factors that lead medical professionals to act, to an extent, autonomously, some trans people are turned away. Ben had just such an experience:

> 'Once when I was 19, I'm 24 now, quite a while ago, I tried to come out to … a GP and that was a really bad experience because I just you know just kind of luck of the draw. Sometimes you get put with people who understand things and sometimes you don't so I got put with somebody who really didn't understand anything I was talking about and was quite rude to me … it was a terrible experience … he started saying really bizarre things. He looked through my file and he saw that my birth dad is from Bahrain and he started asking me like "Oh people over there they … they're not very accepting of gender and stuff like this, they, they don't like women" and all these kind of things, "Is it because your father treated you badly because you were born woman or something like that?" and I was, I was floored. And back then I was not as assertive so I just kind of took it. … I was trying to sort of reach out to this person and be like "I have, I'm having a problem" and they just totally smashed it down. So much so that actually kind of pushed my transition back by quite a few years because I was, I just assumed that what I was gonna get. That was my first experience of it and that's, I guess I assumed that's what I was gonna get going forward so I just didn't kind of, pushed myself back in the closet I guess.' (Ben)

Some trans people have to go through several GPs before they are able to get a referral to a gender identity clinic (GIC) if that's what they are seeking. I argue that this represents the incomplete medicalization of transness. Here, the fact that transness is so highly stigmatized is interfering with its medicalization, so while it is medicalized in all of the ways discussed earlier, it is, ironically, not fully medicalized in the interactional sense since some medical professionals refuse to claim responsibility. When looking at medicalization through a broader lens, however, interactional medicalization remains crucial because while not every medical professional may medicalize trans people, every trans person experiences medicalization, particularly when seeking transition related healthcare.

Deviant versus natural life course medicalized behavior

Another way of understanding medicalized behavior can be with the classification of said behavior as either 'deviant' or conversely as part of a 'natural life course'. The types of medicalized behavior that would be labeled as deviant may seem obvious to cultural insiders but Conrad specifically highlights 'madness, alcoholism, homosexuality, opiate addiction, hyperactivity and learning disabilities in children, eating problems from overeating (obesity) to undereating (anorexia), child abuse, compulsive gambling, infertility, and transexualism, among others' (Conrad, 1992: 213). Transness falls into this category of medicalized deviance, adding a thick layer of social stigma as opposed to the medicalization of a 'natural life process'. Emily commented on this very stigma, remarking that "many of us have stuff from childhood of being told that you're, you know, wrong, different, strange, perverse, whatever else you know, not conforming to what your father wants … peer groups at school all sorts of things". She goes on to say that this very experience of stigma made it more difficult for her to face the gatekeeping and bureaucracy of trans healthcare.[8] On the other hand, there are the 'natural life processes that have become medicalized' which includes 'sexuality, childbirth, child development, menstrual discomfort (PMS), menopause, aging, and death' (Conrad, 1992: 213).

The most distinctive feature of this list is that most of these medicalized natural life processes occur in assigned female at birth (AFAB) people (including the medicalization of childbirth and menstrual cycles) or are socially disproportionately applied to women (such as the medicalization of sexuality and aging), so scholarly and particularly feminist critique of this idea is nothing new. Feminist scholars have long called out the medicalization of natural life processes as a reinforcement of the patriarchy. One critique from Chrisler and Gorman harkens back to a time

> when women's occasional irritability, bloating, and pimple outbreaks were normal experiences, part of the ups and downs of everyday life. In those days (before 1980), people thought that women were angry when there was something to be angry about, irritable because

something was irritating, and tearful because there was reason to be sad. (Chrisler and Gorman, 2015: 77)

Nowadays, these variances, which were once seen as normal, have become medicalized under the labels of premenstrual syndrome (PMS) and premenstrual dysphoric disorder (PMDD), which they argue is a result of the cultural expectation that women always be calm, thus framing their emotions as symptoms. This can be most clearly seen in the symptom lists themselves. There are so many symptoms, especially for PMS, that it is bound to garner a large number of diagnoses. More interesting, though, is that when taken out of context, many of the symptoms (such as craving sweet or salty food) could be part of any normal life course, while others (such as increased sex drive) are considered positive by many 'patients'. Indeed all of these symptoms have one glaring thing in common, which is that they would not be considered symptomatic if they were reported by cis men. Even the more serious diagnosis of PMDD is controversial because it is hard to determine if the depressive state was linked to a pre-existing condition (Chrisler and Caplan, 2002). This critique of natural life course medicalization does not mean the 'issue' doesn't exist, that people don't experience these 'symptoms', rather that medicalizing the 'issue' is not productive and is potentially harmful to the people who experience the medicalized phenomena. In this case it allows for the medically sanctioned stigmatization of people who menstruate and the dismissal of their feelings as valid and normal. This is just one specific example but there are further critiques of the medicalization of pregnancy (Barker, 1998), childbirth (van Teijlingen et al, 2004), sexual desire (Wood et al, 2006), and menopause (Meyer, 2001), in a similar vein.

These arguments are aided in large part by the 'high ground' position of being able to condemn the medicalization of these 'natural life course' events. It is easier to argue for the demedicalization of processes that are common, unavoidable, or are otherwise viewed as 'natural'. Transness on the other hand, according to Conrad, falls into the other category of deviant medicalized behavior and it is the added stigma surrounding this category which complicates critiques of medicalization. Conrad categorizes transness with things like drug and alcohol addiction and child abuse, which is very telling in relation to how transness is viewed socially. Trans people have been, and to many extents still are, seen as deviant, as having something wrong with them. This category of deviance helps to justify their medicalization through framing transness as a problem that medical intervention can solve (Conrad, 1992).

This is a very useful analysis, however I argue that Conrad has missed a category here. I would add to this discourse the category of a 'deviant life course' under which transness (and many other medicalized phenomena) would fall. The exploration and understanding of one's gender identity is a part of the natural life course. It just happens to be a part of life that has a rich history of being suppressed and demonized. In this way transness does not fit into the 'natural life course' category because while people medicalize, for example, pregnancy or menstruation, they are not denying that they are natural phenomena that exist. Transness also does not fit the 'deviant' category simply because it isn't. It makes sense from a sociological point of view but not from the point of view of trans people themselves. Unlike some of the other medicalized phenomena in the deviant category there is nothing about transness that is harmful to others (as is the case with, for example, child abuse) nor anything that is harmful to the person themselves (like with eating disorders). It is simply one possible result of the natural life course event of venturing to understand one's gender which has been labeled deviant by society. The positioning of transness as this deviant life course offers some explanation of why it has become medicalized as well as why proponents of the demedicalization of transness face so many obstacles.

Secularization and medicalization

One theory of medicalization causation that Conrad addresses is the theory of secularization, or the idea that increased medicalization is the result of the gradual cultural shift away from the church as the leading societal authority. This theory states that as society has become less and less centered around a religion (in the case of the UK, Christianity), the authority of science and medicine has swooped in to fill that void. Behaviors that were once classified as sins such as suicide have become reframed as sickness, in this case depression or other mental illness that is understood to cause suicide (MacDonald, 1989). This seems to be a bit of an oversimplification, however. Religion continues to be an influential force in many people's lives and can, along with other forces, wield influence over the medical profession as was the case with the medicalization of homosexuality. In the 1970s, after centuries of homosexuality being labeled both a sin and a mental illness, the harmful effects of those entangled designations were finally widely recognized and homosexuality was gradually demedicalized (Drescher, 2015). The *British Medical Journal* sought to understand the implications of the medicalization and came to the following conclusion:

> Our study shows the negative consequences of defining same sex attraction as a mental illness and designing treatments to eradicate it. It serves as a warning against the use of mental health services to change aspects of human behaviour that are disapproved of on social, political, moral, or religious grounds. (Smith et al, 2004: 3)

This recognizes that even in today's more secularized society, religious and other ideologies can strongly influence which behaviors are labeled as deviant, making those behaviors prone to possible medicalization.

With transness, much of the fierce debate over trans rights has come from some claiming that trans people have a disease that can and should be treated, with others, particularly on the religious right, claiming that they are choosing a deviant lifestyle (of course, many trans people are claiming they are neither diseased nor deviant). The very existence of this debate shows that medicalization has not replaced anything but that there are multiple sources of societal authority coexisting and clashing at once. As Conrad puts it, 'while it is true that medicine is in important ways nudging aside religion as our moral touchstone, the interface of medicine and religion is more complex than a simple secularization thesis would suggest' (1992: 214). Many people when sick will turn to both medicine for treatment as well as prayer or other religious activities.

The nature of the medical profession

There has certainly been a shift in the dominant knowledge producing authority toward the scientific method and the medical profession but its relationship to other authorities and the cause of its rise to dominance remains complex. Another theory involves the nature of the medical profession itself. This posits that the medical profession is purposefully over-medicalizing in order to increase business in an increasingly healthier world (Pawluch, 1983) or to make clinical work less ordinary and routine (Halpern, 1990). Pawluch and Halpern specifically discuss the interesting case of the expansion of the field of pediatrics.

In 'Transitions in Pediatrics: A Segmental Analysis', sociologist Dorothy Pawluch proposes that medicalization has been a crucial life raft for practicing primary care pediatricians in a time when child mortality and morbidity is at an all-time low, in the US in particular. This decrease in child mortality and morbidity is obviously a very positive thing, but with fewer patients to treat Pawluch theorizes that 'primary care pediatricians in the United States survived by broadening the scope of pediatric practice to incorporate the management of children's troublesome behavior' (1983: 450). This represents a medicalization of childhood behavior (or rather misbehavior), and shifting it from the domain of parents, schools, and/or the legal system to the domain of the medical system. These problems include hyperactivity, not fitting in with peers, and struggling academically correlating to new diagnoses like attention deficit disorder (ADD)/attention deficit hyperactivity disorder (ADHD), dyslexia, oppositional defiant disorder (ODD) and others, as well as their corresponding treatments, which can include pharmaceuticals. With this shift, 'the mandate of pediatrics was extended beyond the treatment and prevention of childhood disease to include the positive promotion of child health in all its dimensions' (Pawluch, 1983: 461). This new holistic model of pediatrics has not been universally accepted: many within the medical and academic professions were and continue to be critical of its necessity and potential to do harm with over-diagnosis, however with the perspective of over 20 years since Pawluch wrote about this emerging trend, it is clear to see that it has indeed taken root and become dominant. The notion that medicalization is a natural product of the medical system can help frame the discussion of trans people's experiences with that medical system.

Medical social control

This causation model also fits well with the theory of medical social control. Like any form of social control, medical social control uses certain pressures to enforce societal conformity and medicalization is the tool used to apply those pressures. Conrad highlights four types of medical social control which are specifically used to medicalize deviant phenomena: ideology, collaboration, technology, and surveillance. Medical ideology applies a medical framework to a perceived social problem, as opposed to a religious or a legal ideology being enlisted to deal with that problem. The more that social 'issues' like addiction, aging, and gender variance are explained using a medical ideology and medical discourses, the more that medical ideology becomes one of the dominant social belief systems. Medical collaboration places doctors as decision makers and gatekeepers of things like benefits and jobs. A good example of this is employee drug testing. Medical technology includes the use of pharmaceutical and other interventions. This can be anything from the development of better antidepressants to improvements in prosthetics to new surgical techniques. Medical surveillance is constantly being subject to what Michel Foucault famously called the 'medical gaze', which separates the person's body from the person themselves and highlights the dehumanizing experience of medical observation. The societal perception of this gaze is what gives physicians and other medical professionals much of their clout:

> [I]t was this constant gaze upon the patient, this age-old, yet ever renewed attention that enabled medicine not to disappear entirely with each new speculation, but to preserve itself, to assume little by little the figure of a truth that is definitive, if not completed, in short, to develop, below the level of the noisy episodes of its history, in a continuous historicity. In the non-variable of the clinic, medicine, it was thought, had bound truth and time together. (Foucault, 1973: 54–55)

This gaze is a tool of medicalization and promotes the idea of science and medicine as the dominant societal knowledge producing systems.

With their training and vast experience 'gazing' upon trans bodies, medical professionals are considered the experts on trans people. From the perspective of experiencing the medical gaze, this is something trans people know all too well as they are constantly identified in society and within the medical system by their physical bodies, rather than being allowed to identify themselves, and are time and again reduced down to certain physical characteristics. The value that is placed on the medical gaze devalues the knowledge trans people have of themselves, a knowledge which rejects the body as end-all and be-all and instead is built on lived experience. These forms of medical social control, while having their own negative outcomes such as increased stigma and barriers to accessing services, can seem kinder than other forms of social control. For example, treating people struggling with addiction as sick patients is surely better than treating them as criminals. It often seems like a softer, kinder way of treating the medicalized people. However, legal and medical social controls are too often intertwined, as is the case with the example of drug addiction. With trans people, medicalization is certainly better and kinder than throwing trans people in jail, but medicalization is in many ways just a lesser evil. Other pervasive societal forces are also wrapped up in medical social control, such as ageism and the medicalization of the natural aging process, sexism and the over-medicalization of AFAB people's bodies, and the condemnation of certain 'deviant behaviors' such as transness. The alignment of these societal views with medicalization calls into question the alleged purity of the science based medical system. While it is certainly a powerful tool for social control, if medicalization is indeed so aligned with societal values then it is also susceptible to the shifting of those values and targeted attempts to demedicalize certain phenomena, as I will discuss in the following section.

Demedicalization

As has largely been the case thus far in this discussion, the term medicalization is often used in a critical sense to discuss ways in which aspects of life, personhood, or behavior become unnecessarily labeled as 'illness' which is assigned 'treatments', and the harms that can result. However, any and every illness that is medically treated today has been medicalized. As Conrad says:

> While 'medicalize' literally means 'to make medical' and the analytical emphasis has been on overmedicalization and its consequences, assumptions of overmedicalization are not a given in the perspective. The main point in considering medicalization is that an entity that is regarded as an illness or disease is not ipso facto a medical problem; rather, it needs to become defined as one. (Conrad, 2007: 5–6)

The issue is not simply with medicalization itself but rather with how liberally it is applied. For something to fall into the domain of the medical profession there needs to be an illness with diagnostic criteria and there needs to be a treatment or cure administered by the medical profession. Medicalization is the process of fitting something into that box; some phenomena fit very neatly and others have to be forced in. As one of thousands of possible examples, tuberculosis has been 'medicalized' over hundreds of years as it has been described in medical terms, studied, diagnosed, and treated by the medical profession, but no one is arguing for the demedicalization of tuberculosis. Indeed, some patient advocacy and support groups fight for medicalization, for example, with chronic fatigue syndrome (Broom and Woodward, 1996) or repetitive strain injury (Arksey, 1994). In cases like these patients want medical professionals to recognize, legitimize, and treat seriously their symptoms. The fact that some groups are working toward the medicalization of their experiences while others are arguing for demedicalization is not a contradiction because medicalization is not inherently good or bad. As sociologists Ballard and Elston note, it is simply that 'there seems to be oscillation between medicalisation and demedicalisation of many aspects of everyday life', and that this constant patient-led renegotiating of what should and should not be medicalized is a facet of our post-modern society (2005: 238). Medicalization only becomes problematic when it causes stigma and discrimination and puts up barriers to what becomes labeled as 'treatment'.

With trans people, there is a clear parallel to be drawn between the medicalization of gender variance and the history of the medicalization of sexuality variance. The American Psychiatric Association's Diagnostic and Statistical Manual of Mental Disorders (DSM), while mostly used in the US, is globally influential. From its inception in 1952 until the third edition (DSM-III) removed it in 1973, homosexuality was listed as a psychological disorder. The General Assembly for the World Health Organization (WHO) did not remove homosexuality from the International Classification of Diseases, which is used by the NHS in the UK, until 1990 (Drescher, 2015). This is an example of the medical profession acting in accordance with dominant societal paradigms and later shifting when those paradigms shifted. Conrad refers to this type of process as demedicalization: the undoing of the process of medicalization such that the 'problem is no longer defined in medical terms and medical treatments are no longer deemed to be appropriate solutions' (Conrad, 1992: 224). The idea that homosexuality (and transness) are psychological diseases that can be cured is the exact same ideology that leads to harmful conversion therapy and of course the medicalized model used by the NHS. The NHS model which seeks to 'treat' transness in a way that affirms trans people's gender is of course not as harmful as conversion therapy which rejects trans people's gender and seeks to 'treat' transness through making people cis, however it is the underlying idea that transness requires any type of treatment in the first place that is the issue. In the case of homosexuality, demedicalization was achieved by a concentrated, well-organized political effort which simultaneously challenged the medical system and society as a whole to recognize gay and lesbian people as normal members of that society. It was certainly not easily attained and trans people who want to follow suit with the demedicalization of transness may face an even tougher battle.

The normal and the pathological

The ability to medicalize deviant, abnormal, or pathological phenomena relies on a definition of the pathological and therefore a definition of the healthy or the normal. French physician and philosopher Georges Canguilhem addresses this difficult question in *The Normal and the Pathological*,[9] where disease is partially explained as 'characterized by the fact that it is a reduction in the margin of tolerance for the environment's inconstancies' (1991: 199). Disease or pathology is that which affects someone's ability to be in their world comfortably and competently. While gender doesn't inherently impact one's flexibility within the environment, gender non-conformity can make one unable to blend into that environment.

If that is the pathological then what is its apparent opposite? Canguilhem defines health and physiological norms as such:

> If we acknowledge the fact that disease remains a kind of biological norm, this means that the pathological state cannot be called abnormal in an absolute sense, but abnormal in relation to a well-defined situation. Inversely, being healthy and being normal are not altogether equivalent since the pathological is one kind of normal. Being healthy means being not only normal in a given situation but also normative in this and other eventual situations. What characterizes health is the possibility of transcending the norm, which defines the momentary normal, the possibility of tolerating infractions of the habitual norm and instituting new norms in new situations. (Canguilhem, 1991: 196–197)

The pathological to Canguilhem is not abnormal or the absence of a norm, but rather a new and different type of norm. Therefore 'disease is not merely the disappearance of a physiological order but the appearance of a new vital order' (Canguilhem, 1991: 193). Canguilhem also challenges the temptation to conflate 'normal' and 'typical': 'a human trait would not be normal because frequent but frequent because normal' (1991: 160). To understand this theory through gender diversity we can explain that the pathology of gender identity disorder is just a different way of being gendered, the way that any bodily pathology is just a different mode of embodiment. Being cisgender is the most common state and has therefore become conflated with the normal state when in fact gender variance and gender exploration is also a norm. The issue is not with gender diversity (the 'pathology') but only with the instances and ways in which it causes distress to the person experiencing it.

If the goal of medicalization is to cure the medicalized phenomena and 'in principle, curing means restoring a function or an organism to the norm from which they have deviated' (Canguilhem, 1991: 122), then what is that norm from which a trans person has deviated? Canguilhem goes on to explain that 'the physician usually takes the norm from his knowledge of physiology – called the science of the normal man – from his actual experience of organic functions, and from the common representation of the norm in a social milieu at a given moment' (1991: 122). So the norm is simply that state which is physically and socially common. The influence of the social is crucial here, and Canguilhem stressed that 'in dealing with human norms we acknowledge that they are determined as an organism's possibilities for action in a social situation rather than as an organism's functions envisaged as a mechanism coupled with the physical environment' (1991: 269). As was discussed previously, this came into play with the demedicalization of homosexuality. Medical professionals recognized the shifting social norms at that historic moment which influenced their diagnostic practice. Perhaps transness will similarly come to be seen as normal human variation the way sexual orientation has, medically and more broadly.

A key part of this definitional struggle is finding the line between pathological difference and individual variation. In other words, 'how do we understand the norms peculiar to each species, rabbits, for example, without erasing the slight, fragmentary dissimilarities which give individuals their singularity?' (Canguilhem, 1991: 261). This can partially be achieved by comparing each individual against themselves because 'the borderline between the normal and the pathological is imprecise for several individuals considered simultaneously but it is perfectly precise for one and the same individual considered successively' (Canguilhem, 1991: 182). The resting heart rate of a young Olympic athlete may differ greatly from that of an elderly, sedentary person but neither is pathological for them. If they were to switch heart rates, however, that might be cause for concern. What the specific threshold is for any individual cannot be arrived at objectively: 'it is always the relation to the individual patient through the intermediary of clinical practice, which justifies the qualification of pathological' (Canguilhem, 1991: 229). The pathological is necessarily created through the intervention of clinical practice, through the process of medicalization. The 'patient' is an active agent in this process of the construction of pathology.

[W]e think that medicine exists as the art of life because the living human being himself calls certain dreaded states or behaviors pathological (hence requiring avoidance or correction) relative to the dynamic polarity of life, in the form of a negative value. We think that in doing this living human being, in a more or less lucid way, extends a spontaneous effort, peculiar to life, to struggle against that which obstructs its preservation and development taken as norms. (Canguilhem, 1991: 126)

The agent here determines their own pathological states and struggles against them but always with the input of social norms and with the aid of the medical system. So what then is the fate of an agent trying to redefine their own 'pathology' outside social norms and against the consensus of the medical system?

Challenges from clinicians

Clinicians working in trans healthcare have also shown support for depathologization and potentially even demedicalization. Bouman and Richards have acknowledged that 'while diagnostic terms facilitate clinical care and access to insurance coverage for mental health difficulties in the USA and some other countries, these terms can also have a stigmatising effect' (2013: 165). This is elaborated further in the 2015 paper 'Trans Is Not a Disorder – But Should Still Receive Funding' which is authored by Dr. Richards, Prof. Arcelus, Dr. Bouman, and Dr. Lorimer, as well as Dr. James Barrett, Dr. Leighton Seal, and Dr. Penny Lenihan of London's Tavistock and Portman GIC and Dr. Sarah Murjan of the Nottingham GIC. In this paper, they challenge the need for medicalizing transness with a diagnostic label while acknowledging the specific regulations that bind their practice, namely that they currently cannot provide many treatments without a diagnosis. They explain their position thusly: 'at present, the healthcare funding systems in many countries are set up in such a way as to make it effectively impossible to assist trans people with hormones and surgeries if they do not have a diagnosis which relates to those interventions' (Richards et al, 2015: 310).

They go on to provide an alternative, depsychopathologized model for trans healthcare, which my own argument for demedicalization expands upon. Because they are constrained by these regulations, they specify that 'the political end of removing diagnoses in their entirety is not worth the extraordinary risk of removing the provision of treatment for trans people until such time as alternatives have been put in place' (Richards et al, 2015: 311). This idea of timing is absolutely crucial and I completely agree with the assessment that any depathologization or demedicalization process must come along with changes regarding the regulations that dictate clinicians' practices to ensure there is no loss of access for hormones and surgeries. Finally, they sum up their argument as follows:

> The final question which presents to us, then, is: is diagnosis a useful frame within which to conceptualise trans experience? We submit that it is not. Diagnosis is still necessary for funding and sundry bureaucratic matters, but it is a poor method of understanding the complex interplay of biology, psychology, personal and social influences which form this complex topic; and especially the complex interplay of such elements in any given trans person. Our clinical experience is that understanding and assisting with these elements and the interplay within them is of far more use than the rather procrustean approach of 'fitting' a given trans person within a diagnostic box and potentially dismissing the elements which do not comfortably fit. … We will, of course use diagnosis for pragmatic ends to assist the trans people who see us, but, to help, not to label, and given the long history of pathologisation, and longer history of diversity never as a de facto understanding that trans people are disordered. (Richards et al, 2015: 311)

While they are currently restricted by existing policies and regulations, these clinicians understand the importance of removing limiting and pathologizing diagnostic labels and are working to imagine a future where the care they provide is not limited by such constraints. As Dr. Richards and Dr. Lenihan, along with two colleagues in academia, state: 'In our experience, [clinicians] rarely relish the exercise of power, or the role of "gatekeeper", but they do acknowledge the responsibility of ensuring that people recognize the decisions they are making and so are truly able to give informed consent' (Richards et al, 2014: 255).

The unique challenges of the trans case

The key difference between the medicalization of homosexuality and the medicalization of transness is that interventions that are necessary for many trans people require collaboration with medical professionals. There is nothing that has been labeled as a treatment which requires a diagnosis of homosexuality the way that HRT and certain surgeries require a diagnosis of gender dysphoria. That is where the unique challenge of demedicalizing transness lies. Cis queer people have lobbied for things like better sexual healthcare and proper HIV/AIDS treatment and prevention, but crucially these things were never withheld pending a psychological diagnosis of homosexuality. In this way the medicalization of an illness like HIV/AIDS can be separated from the medicalization of, for example, gay men themselves. The one exception is people who historically have sought to be cured of their homosexuality, however those cases can most often be linked to social and/or medical coercion and conversion therapy is now largely condemned (Smith et al, 2004).

Trans people, on the other hand, are often seeking HRT, psychological therapy, and surgeries, all things firmly claimed by the realm of medicine. It is essential that any argument for demedicalization ensures the continued (and ideally improved) access to these interventions. As Adam describes, the experience of living before having accessed these crucial interventions

> 'makes it so that I am so incredibly uncomfortable on a regular basis you know, it is with me every moment of every day. Like from getting up in the morning and getting in the shower to you know throughout the day wondering if you know my binder is hiding my chest enough and constantly worrying about that to you know wondering if the shopkeeper is gonna think my voice is low enough for a man or if he's gonna misgender me to having to get ready for bed at night and you know take my clothes off again, it is there constantly.' (Adam)

It should not be taken lightly how important it is for people to be able to easily access the hormones and surgeries they need. Currently, in order to access these interventions, they must go through medical gatekeepers and the golden ticket is a diagnosis of gender dysphoria. For transness to become demedicalized by Conrad's definition, not only would transness have to stop being described and understood in medical terms as a 'disorder' but medical treatments would have to no longer be considered 'appropriate solutions'. The first half of this is simple enough to understand as gender dysphoria is already a strange case as it is a diagnosis of request. Ben described that the "therapist will pretty much always give you the go ahead because why not? I don't know … they're very lax I think it's a bit like informed consent … 'Are you trans?' 'Yeah'". Having a disease that you have to seek out to be diagnosed with is certainly not typical, but it is the second half that causes some difficulty. To go through the same channels as homosexuality and fight for the demedicalization of transness without a major change in the medical system or without their cooperation could actually take trans people backwards by endangering access to those 'appropriate solutions' (hormones and surgeries[10]) which are so crucial for many trans people.

This is absolutely critical as the mere fact that trans people themselves seem to freely seek out the diagnosis of gender dysphoria has been used as evidence of its validity.[11] This is a fallacy because the medical system created this diagnosis for a group of people with specific needs and then made it the only avenue for having those needs met; so when trans people seek out a diagnosis of gender dysphoria they are not proving the validity of that diagnosis at all but are rather only proving that, firstly, many trans people want and need therapy, hormones, surgeries, and so on, and secondly that a diagnosis of gender dysphoria is the only way to access those things. The only actual evidence for or against the validity of the diagnosis of gender dysphoria can be found by talking to trans people themselves, a source of knowledge that has been tragically underutilized.

In addition to listening to trans people and valuing their expertise about themselves, for demedicalization to be achieved, the therapy, hormones, and surgeries that are currently labeled as treatments need to be reframed as services while still being made available to trans people. In fact this would increase the people they would be available to as people not seeking a 'traditional' transition path would have easier access in this scenario. This would be incredibly difficult but not as out there as it may seem, especially in countries with greater social safety nets. In the UK and many other countries there are food assistance programs, council housing, state-funded schools, and so on. Of course the effectiveness of these programs in the UK, especially in recent years, can be quite rightly critiqued, but the societal value of providing essential services to those in need is what is relevant. None of these services require a medical diagnosis to access because the services provided have not been claimed by the medical system. If that statement seems unnecessary and if what is and is not claimed by the medical system seems inherent and obvious, then imagine an even more highly medicalized world where food assistance programs require a diagnosis by a nutritionist to access or where admission to school is gate-kept by developmental psychologists. Realms of authority have always been malleable: childbirth has shifted from the responsibility of the community to the responsibility of medicine (van Teijlingen et al, 2004), addiction has moved from purely the realm of the legal system to shared responsibility with the medical system (Tournier, 1985), and homosexuality has moved from the sphere of the legal system to the sphere of the medical system, then became demedicalized, briefly remedicalized during the early years of the HIV/AIDS crises, firmly demedicalized again, and is now in the sphere of the political system (Conrad and Angell, 2004). There is nothing inherent about the gatekeepers society assigns to the access of certain services. In the case of medical services, these gatekeepers come about through processes of medicalization. As I discussed earlier, defining a phenomenon as an illness installs diagnosis as a 'gate' or barrier to accessing what becomes labeled as treatments. This diagnostic process is overseen by relevant medical professionals who become the gatekeepers, either allowing or disallowing people to access 'treatments' (in this case, hormones and surgeries). If the phenomenon is labeled as a mental illness, these professionals will be psychiatrists, psychologists, and other mental health professionals. This medicalized model of transness has been normalized, but if the act of giving hormones and performing surgeries is thought of as a technical skill and the medical professionals who provide them as technicians offering a service rather than curing a disease, there would be no need for this diagnostic process and a lot of the harmful rhetoric around transness would cease to be relevant.

If the stereotypes and misinformation about trans people were no longer being cosigned and perpetuated by the medical system, which as we have seen is a very powerful societal force, then perhaps the rest of society would follow suit. Trans people would no longer be 'sick' people in need of treatment, the binary and linear transition would no longer be the privileged path, and most importantly trans people would no longer have to 'prove' their gender to anyone. This would be a massive change as the current process of acquiring a diagnosis of gender dysphoria requires convincing at least two medical professionals that you are indeed the gender that you claim to be, or more accurately in many cases, that you fit into a highly stereotyped caricature of a binary gender role. It would also remove the need for trans people to socially transition first before accessing these services, which is not safe for everyone to do. Currently, to access a diagnosis of gender dysphoria, people have to start dressing, presenting, and living as their gender (a strange idea that is often poorly defined), even if doing so will render their transness visible in contexts in which being visibly trans is unsafe (such as those described in Erlick, 2019). The phrase 'real life experience' itself also shows a misguided view of what transness is. If gender is something that is inherent, which the medical system seems to think it is as they provide irreversible medical interventions for trans people, then trans people have their whole lifetime worth of 'real life experience'. As discussed in the previous chapter, the medical profession likes to promote the 'trapped in the wrong body' trope, the idea that, for example, a trans woman is a woman trapped in a 'man's body' or that she was born in the wrong body. In other words, that a trans woman requires experience living as a girl/woman before she can be sure she wants to transition.

Real life experience (RLE), as it is used in gatekeeping trans healthcare, refers only to experience playing into the stereotypical role of your gender, or as Ruth Pearce explains, '[underpinning] RLE is the presumption that trans people can and should maintain a consistent (ideally cis-passing) gender identity and gendered appearance' (2018: 200). There is, after all, so much more to the experience of, for example, being a woman than wearing dresses and having a feminine sounding name. Emily said that upon seeing the results of her first appointment with a psychiatrist to get a referral to the GIC she was surprised to see that "the psychiatrist wrote a report out of it, having misheard much of what I said, and an itemized description of what I was wearing, you know … 'the patient presented as female' and in all these little minuscule aspects it was it was interesting to be objectified in that way". This idea of real life experience is especially difficult for non-binary trans people to navigate. They are erased throughout the medical system but it is especially glaring here. What exactly would real life experience look like for a non-binary person? There is no gender role or expectation for being non-binary and most non-binary people can never pass because society at large does not see being non-binary as an option. They are consistently read as either male or female. In my experience it is not even striking some perfect androgynous balance but rather presenting as far away from your assigned gender at birth, so in my case as stereotypically masculine, as possible that gets you taken seriously by the GIC. The very existence of non-binary people challenges a lot of the existing narratives that society and the healthcare system hold about trans people so the fact that they are erased is not all that surprising as they don't fit neatly into existing boxes. It does not make it any less harmful, though, as non-binary people struggle to access transition related healthcare and more generally to navigate a world that is not arranged to fit them. In this case, the medical system operating on a fully informed consent basis and removing diagnosis requirements would improve access to interventions for non-binary people.

Removing diagnosis requirements and the multiple gatekeepers which those requirements bring does not mean that clinicians would play no role. It merely means that their role should be relegated to the very important job of providing whatever care they are expert in with informed consent rather than gatekeeping which consenting people can access that care. But the remaining issue would still be how trans people would go about accessing these services. This is a concern shared by the clinicians providing this care, as I discussed in the Introduction. Most people cannot afford to self-fund their transitions, which can cost tens of thousands of pounds. Some people are able to community fund their surgeries by raising money from friends, family, and even strangers, usually online through social media and sites like GoFundMe, but this is not a viable option for every trans person (Barcelos and Budge, 2019). Why shouldn't these life-saving services be offered to anyone who needs them? One hypothetical reason could be a concern that trans people are just going to change their mind. That allowing, for example, a trans woman to get breast augmentation without going through the lengthy process of referrals and second opinions and so on would be harmful if she ever changed her mind. However, this is a concern that is never leveled at cis women who want to seek breast augmentation for the same reasons. Being able to have breasts has been asserted as a right that all women should have, which we can see from the fact that breast cancer survivors are offered reconstructive breast surgery as standard, so to deny this right to trans women is obviously treating them differently than cis women who do not have breasts. These cis breast cancer survivors do not have to get a second opinion on their gender and prove to the NHS that they are indeed women, so why do trans women? In a similar vein trans men and other transmasculine people run into the same roadblocks when trying to remove their breasts. So perhaps it goes even deeper than the idea that women have the right to have breasts but rather that they must have breasts, so transmasculine people, being seen as women, struggle to access double mastectomies. Dan explained it as follows:

> 'And actually going privately one of the things that I found absolutely absurd was that in order to have the double mastectomy I needed to take in … a letter saying that I was of sound mind to have that surgery but if I wanted to be Jordan[12] and have an enlargement that was like twice the size of my head fine they would have given it to me you don't have to have any kind of checks for that and I remember saying to quite a few places like that is ridiculous.' (Dan)

Dan perfectly highlights the frustration of being treated differently than people seeking similar procedures simply because his procedure was related to his transness. Sometimes our bodies have and/or lack things that cause extreme distress and rectifying that is a valid use of biotechnology that should be available to all on an informed consent basis.[13] People changing their mind after these procedures or de-transitioning is thought to be quite rare, but even if de-transitioning were a major concern, the way to address it would not be the adding of more gatekeepers. It would be to tackle the horrible social stigma that plagues people who do not 'pass', to not force people to choose between a linear, binary transition or none at all, and to increase access to these interventions so detrans people (people who once identified as trans but no longer do, see Hildebrand-Chupp, 2020) can access them as well.

There is certainly some progress that has been made, and Ruth Pearce notes that the NHS is already moving toward depathologization,[14] although not quite demedicalization. The depathologization movement 'can be understood as primarily concerned with depsychopathologisation: its proponents don't want to remove access to medical interventions for transitioning individuals, but rather aim to see trans health being understood and treated differently' (Pearce, 2018: 185). George echoed this in our conversation when he asserted, "I don't think it's a mental health issue at all I think it's totally separate but, it's so difficult to get [psychiatrists] to separate it in their minds". Demedicalization, on the other hand, takes it a step further. As opposed to depathologization, which seeks to stop labeling transness as a mental illness but to continue requiring a diagnosis of some sort to access certain interventions, demedicalization seeks to redefine these interventions as not inherently medical at all.[15] It is moving from being medicalized as a mental illness to being medicalized as a physical illness or perhaps as some other category of illness versus ceasing to be medicalized at all. Thus the existing progress that Pearce has identified, while very positive, can best be labeled as depathologization, not demedicalization. Trans healthcare providers are openly recognizing that transness is not a mental disorder and that non-binary and fluid gender experiences are increasingly being recognized within trans healthcare:

> The depathologisation movement has therefore seen several successes in the UK, including shifts away from pathologisation in gender clinic care pathways, somewhat more progressive national protocols for Scotland and England, and possible amendments to legal gender recognition. These changes have been made possible through extensive negotiation both within the UK and on an international level. They rely upon a restructuring of macro-level power relations through the establishment of trans knowledges as credible. However, the delivery of gender identity services in the UK continues to rely on an extensive process of gatekeeping, which broadly maintains the micro-level power differentials between practitioner and patient. (Pearce, 2018: 192–193)

These successes are certainly to be celebrated but, as Pearce noted, there is a long way to go, namely by removing gatekeeping. Removing the diagnosis of gender dysphoria but continuing to offer services to those trans people who require them within an informed consent model[16] would remove these gatekeepers and could go a long way toward the destigmatization of trans people in the same way that the demedicalization of homosexuality did. It would certainly be an uphill battle but I look forward to a day when the medicalization of transness is viewed to be as outdated as the medicalization of homosexuality is generally viewed today.

5

Bureaucracy, time, and space

> Plumbing is not gender-neutral.
> Crawford (2015: 65)

In this chapter I build upon the previous chapter by looking at three functions of social control as they are present in the lives of trans people in the UK: bureaucracy, time, and space. The data and theorization presented here supports existing work by Preciado, Vincent, Naugler, Pearce, Adam, Israeli-Nevo, Crawford, and Munt and extends that by Varela, Brown et al, and Maister to apply to gender, transness, and transition related healthcare. Specifically I focus on the varied elements of the medical bureaucracy which prevent trans people from accessing quality healthcare, waiting and wait times, waiting rooms, and bathrooms. In different ways a lack of control over each of these elements block trans people from good health and in combination they highlight the dire state of trans healthcare in the UK.

Bureaucracy

Framing trans healthcare as a bureaucracy illuminates many of the structural barriers trans people face. The bureaucracies I am describing here are all the National Health Service (NHS) and private healthcare pathways that trans people encounter and the relationship between those pathways, primarily General Practitioner (GP) surgeries, gender identity clinics (GICs), and mental health services. Just the prospect of having to engage with these bureaucracies can be enough to dissuade people from advocating for themselves. For example, George describes not pushing his GP surgery when they continued to have his title wrong in the system, an experience I have also had.

> '[W]hen you feel like you're climbing up this massive hill, you let the little things go sometimes. Which you shouldn't because they do make you feel really bad and I dread my name coming up on that screen cause everybody's gonna be like "What?". I just hope people think it's like an admin error, cause it's difficult when I go to pick my prescriptions up and it's actually Ms. you know it's just strange, very strange.' (George).

In addition to this sort of general challenge, there are certain features of these bureaucracies; cancelled appointments, the exercise of ticking boxes, having to jump through hoops,[1] and the shifting of responsibility, that have been flagged by the participants as points of frustration for trans people. Of course these bureaucratic features will be found throughout many healthcare services, but accessing transition related healthcare increases some trans people's exposure to these bureaucracies. Furthermore, some features are more present in trans healthcare, as I will discuss in this chapter, such as the shifting of responsibility, which is exacerbated by a lack of understanding from GPs and other healthcare providers about GICs and how they operate.

Cancelled appointments

A specific complaint about the system was appointments being cancelled at the last minute. Dan experienced this issue when he organized regular appointments at the request of the psychiatrist only to have that schedule disrupted by delayed and cancelled appointments. He explains:

> 'She gave me an array of times and she said "Probably monthly's better" and I was like "Yeah yeah monthly's good". And then I got an appointment two months later and you're just kind of like wait, you said monthly … so it was like literally, say the beginning of August I had an appointment, the next wasn't booked until like the end of September, no middle of October, and then there was supposed to be another one booked for December which got cancelled.' (Dan)

He experienced a disconnect between the care that he expected, the care the doctor said was appropriate, and the care he actually received, both through appointments not being available monthly and then through the appointments that were booked being cancelled. He has also had two other appointments at the GIC cancelled, one far in advance but with no explanation and one very last minute.

> 'So I was supposed to be there for 2:30, they phoned me up at nine o'clock in the morning was like, "We wanted to let you know because you travel from so far away", okay great, fantastic. So I've already waited and now I'm not getting the appointment, and never mind the fact that I was supposed to have this physical on the same day so they've already cancelled the physical … in fairness that was three months' notice they gave me on this physical being cancelled due to unforeseen circumstances. It's not that unforeseen if you can let me know three months before which was my exact response to them. … It's not unforeseen it's foreseen three months away. … They didn't tell

me what the problem was so then it's just like "We're not gonna tell you that simple honest answer".' (Dan)

He is frustrated both by the appointment that was cancelled in advance because of the GIC's failure to provide an explanation as well as the appointment that was cancelled on the morning of the appointment. This is also a problem with other health services. Flora discussed their experience of Children and Adolescent Mental Health Services as follows:

> 'I started off there but I literally quit after three sessions because they would cancel on me. Like I'd get there and they would cancel my appointment then and there, or sort of say "It's cancelled" and then I would cry and then the guy would come out and give me my appointment anyway.' (Flora)

The healthcare Flora was accessing here was not specifically gender related, but the issue of cancelled appointments was still prevalent and distressing.

Ticking boxes

Another feature of these bureaucracies is the idea of ticking boxes. Having gatekeeping practices in place that are purely exercises in going through the motions. When Dan was at an appointment he saw as unnecessary he asked the doctor what the purpose of the appointment was and the doctor replied to "just basically tick boxes". Another participant described her first appointment as follows:

> 'It was an assessment by the senior and their old school psychiatrist who barked questions and it was more, it was a tick box exercise, yeah. And for those expecting psychotherapy it was roughly the opposite. And I know people who think mental health services are there for your mental health therefore to expect some sort of caring, might be didactic but it would be caring, and what they got was the opposite you know basically it's the gatekeeping exercise of "Are you real?".' (Emily)

Emily is experiencing a disconnect between transness being labeled as a mental health issue, and thus gender services being connected to mental health services, and the care she actually received. She expected psychotherapy or at least a 'caring' encounter but instead was met with having to tick the right boxes to prove her realness. Another participant, Ben, discussed being very aware of having to tick the boxes during his private gender services appointment to the point of, in his words, lying to make sure he ticked those boxes. When I asked him if he felt he had to say or imply that he wanted top and bottom surgery to access hormones he said:

> 'I don't think anyone mentioned top surgery and bottom surgery and all that stuff but it was definitely … it was expected I think, although it wasn't really expressly said so I just went with that. I, I just kind of gauged what they were doing and it seemed like when I was being assessed that's what they were looking for, just ticking boxes. I think he was literally ticking boxes as I was going … so I just looked at that and I just thought "Okay I'm just gonna …", you know, cause I didn't go in there thinking I'm gonna lie through my teeth … I kind of just got in there and I thought "Ugh this environment is a little bit like intimidating I'm just gonna see how it goes" and then that's what it was.' (Ben)

Due to the person assessing him ticking off boxes, Ben omitted the fact that he does not identify as a binary man and does not want a linear, binary transition because he was worried that if he did not tick those boxes he would be denied the testosterone he was seeking. Paul B. Preciado noted a similar feature of the French medical bureaucracy, that 'in order to legally obtain a dose of synthetic testosterone, it is necessary to stop defining yourself as a woman' (2013: 60). This was not something they were willing to do so they self-medicated instead. People knowing what the boxes are (or thinking they know what the boxes are) and having no other choice but to make sure they tick them to access the care they require reinforces to the bureaucracy that their boxes are accurate.

Having heard many stories similar to those the participants have relayed, I arrived at my GP well prepared to tick the necessary boxes and jump through whatever hoops would be placed in front of me (another feature I discuss in this chapter). A friend who had gone through the process before sent me the list of questions, the literal boxes that the GP would have to fill out, so I could prepare my answers. I went into the appointment with my guard up but my GP was quite supportive as they had done this before with another patient at the practice. They had printed out the list of questions for the Charing Cross clinic but I corrected that I wanted to be referred to the Northampton clinic so they printed out that sheet (the one I had studied) and went down the line asking me each question. I answered them slowly but briefly so my GP could copy down my answers. All in all it took about 10–15 minutes. What struck me more than anything going through this process was how unnecessary it all felt. The questions asked were the same ones that are rehashed in the first appointment at the GIC so providing the information did not feel productive. It was essentially a self-referral by proxy. The only difference I experienced between, say, when I referred myself for physical therapy to this referral experience was who actually filled out the form. My GP merely copied my answers down word for word so their only function in this exchange is an authority given to them by the NHS to tick these boxes. An authority that is not extended to me as the trans person seeking access to the GIC. I have the authority to refer myself to the physiotherapist but not to the gender clinic (I address this further in the upcoming section on forms).

Jumping through hoops

In our conversation, Dan described how he struggled to find out what hoops he had to jump through in the first place. His case is different from the 'usual' NHS care path as he went on testosterone and had top surgery privately while on the waiting list for the GIC, so by the time he was seen he was only seeking lower surgery. He explained that at Charing Cross there was specific guidance on what the process entailed and what appointments he needed to have for what reasons and in what order, but even after being seen at his clinic (Northampton) he remarked: "I still didn't know what the hell I was doing." He asked his psychiatrist at the clinic who told him another doctor would make it clear at his physical.

> 'So I drive up for a physical, guy rocks up late which annoys me. Anyway we start talking, "Is this your first appointment?" I'm like "Okay." Then he tells me … "Oh I don't know why they booked you in for a short appointment you need a much longer one for a physical." He said "Are you only here for this?" and I was like "Yup." And he must have been able to tell by that point that I'd lost all interest in being there. Right now the only thing that he could do was give me the answers on what hoops I need to jump through, so I'm like "I feel like a flea, tell me what hoop I need to jump through and I'll do it" and so then he turns around and he's like "Oh well I suppose you don't really need it we normally do it as first before we get on testosterone" … so I'm just kinda like "Well okay so why do I need to do it now?" and he goes "just basically tick boxes" and he was like "but I don't think we need to do it", blah blah blah.' (Dan)

Dan felt that he was being rushed through the appointment, which he later attributed to there being confusion around him having a referral for another mental health service and them thinking he was going to be leaving their care. Although he has now resigned himself to having to jump through hoops, he is not happy about the process and he at least wants the hoops to be clearly laid out for him, so he is further annoyed when that is not the case. The clinic failed to communicate to Dan what exactly he could expect and what was expected of him and they attempted to shift the responsibility onto another service. Carey also described their experience of getting referred to the GIC in a similar way, remarking that:

> '[I]n Wales, they still have the hoop that you have to jump through where you, instead of just going to see your GP and getting referred to the gender clinic you go see your GP, then you go see a psychiatrist, and then they refer you to the gender clinic.' (Carey)

This extra hoop has also impacted George's life. He is from Wales but told me that "the main reason why I moved to England is because in Wales they have no gender identity clinic".[2] Him and his partner want to move back to Wales but he does not want to jeopardize his place on the waiting list.

In addition to delaying and complicating healthcare for trans people, some of these 'hoops', such has having to get two signatures for lower surgery, are also frustrating for the clinicians enforcing them. Dr. Walter Bouman, Dr. Christina Richards, and Prof. Jon Arcelus, three clinicians from the Nottingham GIC, along with many international colleagues, have questioned the need for two referrals, or 'signatures', for lower surgery in their 2014 paper 'Yes and Yes Again: Are Standards of Care which Require Two Referrals for Genital Reconstructive Surgery Ethical?'. As that paper states:

> The purpose of the second opinion is not discussed or clarified in any of the current [Standards of Care], despite the fact that obtaining the second opinion can cause delays in treatment, especially in sparsely populated areas, and may be seen by some as unduly invasive. Indeed, in the broader field of medicine aside from trans services, there are very few cases in which two opinions for physiological interventions are required and those which do mostly involve people who lack capacity to consent to treatment or people who are seen outside of a multidisciplinary team. (Bouman et al, 2014: 379)

They highlight that concerns such as the irreversibility of the procedures and the 'loss of healthy tissue' are often cited as a reason for needing two signatures for lower surgery. However, they counter that:

> [A] further argument ... is that of the number of signatures required to allow other irreversible elective surgeries such as live kidney donation, and cosmetic facial, breast and genital surgery, for example. In such cases (when not related to gender dysphoria), either a single or no psychiatric or psychological opinion is required, often at the discretion of the operating surgeon. (Bouman et al, 2014: 381)

Bouman and Richards also note in a 2013 paper that '[i]t is significant that, with the exception of some neurosurgery for psychiatric symptoms, no other surgical intervention requires the production of two written opinions' (2013: 169). These gatekeeping practices are currently required of clinicians but those cited here (and likely other colleagues of theirs) are challenging their necessity and usefulness.

Shifting responsibility

This feature of bureaucracy that some participants picked up on of shifting responsibility comes into play when overworked services appear loathe to take on patients that they see as already being under the care of another service. Adam, who was struggling with mental health issues not related to his gender, sought therapy to deal with those issues while he was on the waiting list for the GIC. His GP was encouraging him to wait to see the psychiatrist at the GIC[3] but he was insistent that he needed outside help and got on the waiting list for his local mental health service. He explains his experience with this as follows:

> 'I went in and spoke to someone from the [mental health team], and you know they did the same thing that basically this GP ended up doing which was, you know, they kept kicking the football back to … the gender clinic. "Oh the gender clinic will have psychological services so why not wait until …", you know and they knew that what I needed in terms of that aspect of my mental health, what I needed was trauma therapy, and they were assuming that that was something that was gonna be on offer at the gender clinic. And I kept saying "I really don't think that's the way it's set up from like what I've read about on their website I think it's just that you can get psychological, like you can get therapy for your gender issues like if you're having a hard time coming to terms with your gender you can get therapy for that but I don't think that they offer trauma therapy or any therapy that's not related to gender issues." "Oh well wait and see," you know that type of thing.' (Adam)

Adam later ended up having what he described as a nervous breakdown and requiring emergency mental health services. Dan also sought the care of his local mental health team because, as he said, "if I'm gonna get problems sorted out then all good I've got a whole new body I actually wanna live, I wanna live without a whole load of mental problems afterwards" (Dan). Here he is framing the mental health services and the GIC as both essential but very different services. The GIC is helping him get his "whole new body" while the mental health services are helping him live free from "a whole load of mental problems" in that new body. When he got through to the local mental health team, they tried to refer him to the GIC. He informed them he was already under the care of a GIC but they told him his problems were too gender related. Vincent highlights this very issue in their guidance for mental health providers:

> It is vital that mental health practitioners do not refuse trans clients on the assumption that they are not qualified or equipped to address issues that could be (or could be related to) dysphoria. There is no reason why a mental health provider cannot work with a trans person to assist with mental health prior to (if sought), during, or after a medical transition process. (Vincent, 2018: 75).

Even if Dan's mental health problems were related to gender, he should not have been refused mental healthcare on that basis. After being turned away from his local mental health team, he made an appointment to discuss these issues with the psychiatrist at the GIC but was told by them that his problems weren't "gender enough". Just like Adam he describes feeling desperate for someone to accept the responsibility of helping him, as he said, "all my problems are gender until I go to the gender identity clinic and then they're not gender enough … where in actual fact I just wish someone would acknowledge that all my problems are mine and I really don't want them to be problems anymore" (Dan).

All of these experiences Dan has had have led to an overall frustration with the lack of care bring provided by these systems:

> 'I paid into a system with the understanding that I was paying into something that would help me. If it wasn't gonna help me, regardless of whether or not I paid into it, then at least damn well tell me right from the start "We're not gonna help you this isn't what we cover" and then I can go someplace else, but don't keep throwing me about.' (Dan)

These experiences demonstrate a bureaucratic instinct to shift responsibility to other services. One facet that enables this shifting responsibility is the deep compartmentalization of the mental health services. Due to the highly specialized identity of the GICs, their existence allows for anyone questioning their gender to be separated from the more general mental health services. Additionally, there seems to be a misunderstanding of what the other services do. An assumption that 'you get this help elsewhere' when that's not necessarily the case as well as an assumption that people only have one 'issue'. In Adam's case the assumption was that all his issues were gender related and that he could get help for all his issues at the GIC when in fact he needed help from the GIC for transition related healthcare but also happened to have separate trauma issues and required additional support from mental health services. These misunderstandings, assumptions, and shifting responsibilities are resulting in trans people not receiving the care they need.

Forms

Another common feature of any bureaucracy is its paperwork. In the case of the NHS, the referral forms for different services can illuminate how those services are understood and what level of gatekeeping is at play. In the following sections I will look at referral forms for the two different GICs[4] used by participants alongside referral forms for a physiotherapy service, a local mental health service, and 'female breast reduction'.

Self-referral

As I discussed earlier, my experience of filling out the GIC referral form with my GP felt like a self-referral by proxy. Comparing the form my GP and I collaborated to fill out to refer me to the GIC with the form I filled out to refer myself to physical therapy about a year prior shows some interesting distinctions. The first major difference is that the GIC referral form was 12 pages while the physical therapy referral was only three. The first couple of pages of the GIC referral form were directed at the GP, explaining the process, outlining the NHS best practice, and reminding them that 'GPs must co-operate with GICs and gender specialists in the same way that you would co-operate with other specialists'. This would be completely unnecessary in the physical therapy form as there has been a gatekeeper removed (the GP) so there is no need to provide these instructions to said gatekeeper. This is followed by a patient consent section which was also notably absent from the physical therapy form. In fact I did not even need to sign the physical therapy referral and simply emailed it to the service.

A positive feature of the GIC referral form was its awareness of gender and sex. While the physical therapy form only had 'male' or 'female' to check, the GIC form asked for 'Assigned Sex (at birth)' with a blank space which would allow intersex people to specify their sex in a more detailed way. The GIC form also asked for more biographic information that the physical therapy form did not require, specifically age and religion. Both forms asked for ethnicity but the physical therapy form specifically stated that it was optional while the GIC form did not. After the biographical information, both forms asked for a description of the reason for referral, with the GIC form specifically asking for a 'detailed' description and allotted far more space for each question. While the physical therapy form asked a bit about employment and activity, which are specifically relevant to that type of issue, the GIC form asked for 'Current Circumstances (Details of current living arrangements, on-going physical, social, financial concerns, support networks, relevant history, childhood, education, relationships, occupation)', which is difficult to relate to the care the GIC will be providing. These differences in length, thoroughness, and types of questions asked highlight the additional gatekeeping practices the NHS bureaucracy has in place for gender services and how it might look different as a true self-referral process.

Mental health services

A potential explanation for the thorough assessment of 'current circumstances' and mental health history and status in the GIC referral forms could be because the GIC is in some ways treated like a mental health service. However, when comparing these GIC referral forms to the referral form for a mental health service accessed by one of the participants, both the GIC referral forms asked for more detailed mental health information than the referral to mental health service. One GIC form even had a section for 'forensic history', something that was not deemed relevant to include in the mental health service form. Much like the 'current circumstances' section on the other GIC form it is difficult to see the use of this section when providing people with transition related healthcare. Trans people are consistently being asked to provide more information and to go through a more stringent process to access their care than people seeking similar services that are not trans specific.

Breast reduction

Surgery that is labeled cosmetic is generally not provided on the NHS, however there are a few exceptions. If someone can show that their breasts are too large and are causing them pain (and that they have tried and failed to use non-surgical interventions), they can apply for funding for a breast reduction. As sociologist and gender scholar Diane Naugler explains in 'Crossing the Cosmetic/Reconstructive Divide: The Instructive Situation of Breast Reduction Surgery': 'The pursuit of (government or insurance industry paid) breast reduction surgery in Canada, the United States, and Britain is currently acted out under the rubric of illness. As such, emotional and aesthetic concerns are seen as secondary to physical complaints' (2009: 229).

Essentially, one must prove that they are seeking this 'cosmetic' procedure for non-cosmetic reasons. This is an incredible hurdle to clear, especially within the NHS where this surgery is not funded through the normal pathways. Even with this difficulty, the referral form for this procedure considered by one participant is very brief and straightforward. There were no questions about the patient's mental health, criminal history, or living situation. If a transmasculine person wants a complete breast reduction (double mastectomy) with the NHS, they have to provide all of this information, wait to access the GIC, then make it through the process of accessing top surgery.[5] Once again, the referral process for the trans specific healthcare is more invasive than the similar procedures that are targeted toward cis people.[6] In this case, what trans people are seeking sits at the border of the reconstructive/cosmetic divide. Trans people cannot use physical complaints to access a double mastectomy. They may have mental/emotional distress and/or aesthetic concerns but, as Naugler highlights, those are not given as much weight. The very idea of a reconstructive/cosmetic divide itself 'elides its own dependence on notions of normalcy and gendered embodiments' (Naugler, 2009: 235). It is this idea of a normally gendered body with, in this case, the appropriate absence or presence of breasts, which trans people are disrupting when accessing top surgery, hence the additional bureaucratic hurdles.

Bureaucracy as a social network

In 'Intimate Distances: Fragments for a Phenomenology of Organ Transplantation', Chilean biologist and philosopher Francisco Varela recounts the process of getting a liver transplant. Varela describes this medical bureaucracy as a 'complex social network', a concept that translates onto the GIC system (2001: 260). Like the elaborate bureaucracy that gave Varela someone's liver, the GIC system too is a complicated web of different actors, agencies, and paperwork that one must be fairly adept to navigate. Entwined in this social network are GPs, GICs, psychiatrists, endocrinologists, surgeons, other care providers, receptionists, pharmaceutical manufacturers, the federal government, policy makers, trans people, and so on. Each play a role and interact with the other actors to make this system run and each can play a role in the ways it shifts and changes over time.

There are two distinct hierarchies within this social network, one between doctors and patients, and another among patients. In the doctor–patient relationship the doctor has the authority of their education and position as expert. Varela highlights this when discussing how, as liver transplant patients, they have asserted that they can feel their livers while doctors insist that that is impossible. There is a disagreement between the doctor's expertise and the patient's expertise as the person living through the experience. This relationship is even more complex in the GIC system as the patient often must be the expert, educating doctors to access the care they want. Furthermore they must be the expert on what the doctor's expertise is so they can line up with the doctor's knowledge in order to be accepted as trans and given the care they are seeking.[7] Among patients Varela experienced privilege in terms of class, location, and even living in a time when this treatment is available. These privileges are at play in trans healthcare as well. Those with greater financial resources can pay to access private healthcare and people living in certain parts of the country have easier access to GICs and GPs willing to refer them to those GICs. People who have accessed transition related healthcare at different points in time have had different levels of ease accessing that care and greater or lesser wait times.

Time

Wait times

A defining feature of transition related healthcare in the UK is waiting, or as one participant Emily called it, "marking time in the system". This waiting primarily takes place on the waiting list for a GIC but it can also take the form of waiting for psychiatrist appointments, therapy, hormones, surgery, and waiting to be able to reach out to get the initial referral from the GP in the first place. This waiting can differ based on two key factors, financial resources and geographic location. If people have the financial resources they can go private which greatly shortens the wait time for whatever care they are trying to access. As Ruth Pearce observed when discussing trans temporalities, 'the financial costs of private treatment and/or the possible risk of self-medication are typically regarded as preferable to the uncertainty of waiting' (2018: 150, my emphasis). Each GIC also has a different wait time so depending on where someone lives and which GIC is closest to them they may wait different amounts of time for their appointments, although some people in England who are able to travel may try and get referred to a GIC farther away if they know it has a shorter wait time.

In 'Waiting for a Liver Transplant', Brown et al describe the changing emotions of people on the liver transplant list, starting with feeling blessed and happy to get past the first hurdle and get on the list followed by discouragement as time goes on and fear of surgery once they get closer (as well as guilt that someone will have to die for them to live). Many of the participants discussed a similar trajectory, feeling happy and excited to get on the GIC waiting list but disappointed upon realizing how long they would have to wait until the next step as well as fear of not being accepted as trans enough or being denied the care they are seeking after all that waiting. During this process of waiting, Brown et al observed that everyone on the waiting list thought about time but in their own ways, 'time is experienced both as "moving very fast" and stretching out all at once' (2006: 130). Time spent waiting is a liminal space distinct from their past before they were on the waiting list and separate from the future they are hoping for after they have finished waiting.

> They are the people of the List. They are denizens of a strange land with dark terrain, where time speeds up and slows down in rhythm with the imaginatively felt signs of closeness or distance from transplantation,

their own private eschaton[8] … time on waiting lists is a time apart from the narrative of their lives. Those waiting feel held up or on hold in a purgatory with its own clock. … It is a time of utter subjectivity. … Despite the initial sense of elation and gratitude that accompany being placed on the transplant list, in time, depression and emotional lability are common to the experience and arise out of a sense of frustration of other goals. (Brown et al, 2006: 132)

The time spent in this liminal space, in this 'passivity of patient hood' as Brown et al call it, always looking toward the future, takes a toll on people's mental health and is exactly the type of waiting that the trans people I interviewed described experiencing as they waited/wait for months and even years to even begin to access transition related healthcare.

There are several episodes of waiting that someone transitioning may experience. Waiting, for various reasons, to seek out a referral from one's GP, waiting for the first GIC appointment, waiting to be approved for hormones, waiting for the prescription to come through, waiting for the physical changes of hormones, waiting to be approved for various surgeries, waiting for those surgeries, waiting to fully recover, and so on, however I will primarily focus on waiting for one's first GIC appointment as that is often the longest and most fraught wait. Many participants were surprised by how long that initial wait time was, both because they were not told explicitly how long the wait would be and because it was significantly longer than the 18 weeks the NHS promises. Emily, who went through the referral process in England when the English care path still required going through a mental health team as an intermediary, described her experience as follows:

'It was a six-month wait or so before, because the mental health team were, I think it was longer than six months might have been eight months, it was a long time. Basic problem was the mental health team had only one person they believed was competent to make a judgement on gender stuff and they were away on secondment or holiday or whatever else and that meant they were booked up.' (Emily)

She ended up waiting longer than she expected because of limited staff and something as arbitrary as one employee being away. Adam was referred more recently so was able to get direct referral from his GP and explained his experience:

'Unfortunately the waiting times for to access NHS treatments in England for gender therapy were just quite long and it took longer than anyone expected it was going to. Being referred in September of last year and they received the referral at the end of September and that's when the sort of clock starts ticking, and you know according to NHS guidelines it's supposed to be, you're supposed to be seen within 18 weeks of once that clock starts ticking, so a little over four months maybe five months, and from the time that I was referred it took them six months to even notify me about when my appointment was gonna be and then my appointment ended up being ten months after. And the wait times when I was referred were three and a half/four months so it's been about twice as long, nearly three times as long as everybody expected it was gonna be.' (Adam)

Adam is acutely aware of both the NHS guidelines for how long he should have waited as well as the GIC's published wait times when he was referred and he was still waiting far longer than he expected. He places the blame for these long wait times not on the NHS itself but on the government for not providing enough funding. As he sees it, "they're just trying to do the best that they can with what they've got so I can't fault them" (Adam). Carey explained how the waiting makes them feel "kind of crap":

'I had to wait seven months for my … first appointment with the chronic pain management service and that was just a nightmare, and I know that this is gonna be longer than that for something that effects my life just as much if not more so it's frustrating. And it's frustrating not knowing how long the waiting list is right know like I've been looking at figures that are kind of from last year and that are approximations and I have no idea whether there's been a sudden spike at this point of people being referred so it's yeah I'm impatient. I like to know how long I'm gonna be waiting and yeah just not knowing and not knowing how long everything's gonna, you know this is the waiting time until my first appointment I have no idea how long after that it will be until I potentially am able to get top surgery so it could be like three years and I've already been living with this discomfort without having spoken to my doctor about it for three or four years so we're talking like the same length of time again potentially until I can feel comfortable in my body which I try not to think about too much because it makes me very sad.' (Carey)

They have experienced waiting for healthcare before so they know a bit of what to expect and are experiencing stress both at the prospect of a long wait as well as not knowing how long the wait will be.

Navigating unclear wait times

With several participants there was confusion around how long the wait list was and what kind of communication they should be receiving from the GICs. Many participants discussed calling or emailing their GIC to try and find out more information, often unsuccessfully. Carey was awaiting a confirmation letter from their GIC but actually found out they were on the waiting list from a different clinic. They went in for a routine blood test and was told by the nurse that the GIC had also requested their bloods. This was the first they had heard of being on the GIC's radar and at the time of our conversation they had still not received a letter, "I am still waiting for a letter from [the clinic] saying welcome to the waiting list, and maybe I won't get one I don't know" (Carey).

Other participants knew about the long wait times and tried to navigate them. I was warned about them by my GP when I went to get my referral. I was told "Well, you know this won't be happening any time soon", that the wait times were very long, with a tone of discouragement as if they were saying "Are you sure you want to bother?". About a month after that appointment, in March 2017, I received a letter from the GIC acknowledging my referral and stating I was now on the clinic waiting list. I received my first appointment in October of 2019. While the incredible length of the wait was not surprising to me it was still distressing. Adam, who also struggled with the wait, accessed private gender therapy while he was on the GIC waiting list. Dan asked to be referred to the GIC that had the shortest wait time at the time he was seeking a referral. His GP however accidentally sent the referral to a different clinic so he got behind when the referral had to be changed. The stated waiting time came and went with no appointment and he called many times before eventually being told that he would be waiting an unknown amount of time but that it would be many months longer than he thought. After receiving this update he went private for his hormone therapy and later for top surgery to shorten the wait. I also accessed top surgery privately after waiting for years in the NHS system. After several repetitive appointments I was finally referred for top surgery in June 2021, being told that while they couldn't say how long the wait for surgery would be it wouldn't be "sooner than three years". Faced with this wait I figured out how I would fund private surgery and transferred my referral to the same surgeon's private list in September 2021.

Another participant, Flora, did not even bother with the NHS and went straight for private care. They explained their concern over long wait times as well as the idea that the waiting might be for nothing:

'Just as long as I can remember I've heard terrible things about trans healthcare with the NHS and waiting lists and sort of the fact that they, stuff like they send you letters instead of emails and it just seemed like I would be waiting a very long time and I would be incredibly unhappy and sort of I guess I am privileged enough to be able to pay for private healthcare so I thought why wouldn't I. … I worried that I'm just not binary enough … I was just really scared that I just wouldn't be believed so I could be on a waiting list for like two years and then sort of be turned away and yeah I just thought to myself if testosterone turns out to be an absolutely terrible idea at least I haven't had to wait for two years to be on it.' (Flora)

For Flora, waiting a long time was not even an option since they were able to go private. They did note however that wait times have gone up for private care too, they waited five months between their initial appointment and seeing the endocrinologist to confirm their testosterone prescription (although they had a bridging prescription during that time). I waited just over a year between transferring my referral to the surgeon's private waiting list and my actual top surgery. On the contrary, another participant who went private described being shocked at how quickly he was able to get testosterone:

'I just looked it up online. I don't really, don't know how I found it, it was kind of like completely out of the blue. I had this impression that if you want to be on HRT [hormone replacement therapy] it's gonna take forever and you have to wait and everything like that and I was just searching around one day and I just found it and it was kind of like too good to be true I didn't really believe it. And then I just went through that and it was it was pretty good actually you can have it very fast.' (Ben)

In this case he knew about the long wait times for NHS care and was pleasantly surprised when he found out how quick accessing private care could be.

In addition to the strategies of being aware of different wait times to get referred to the GIC with the shortest waiting list and going private, Carey describes a different perspective on potentially inadvertently 'skipping the queue'.

'I end up with a lot of like chest pain quite a lot and I'm always like I need to go and see [my GP] to make that this is the normal thing not something different, but every time that happens I'm like "Oh hmm but if I, if I did have breast cancer maybe I could get a double mastectomy like sooner than I would through the other services." Which makes me feel like crap because I'm literally like "Huh, hmm, maybe if I had cancer I could get this soon", that's not how normal people think. I have at least one other non-binary friend who has had the same thing happen, two other non-binary friends who have had the same thing happen, and it's like a real genuine fear as well I'm like "Oh my god what if I have cancer", but then I'm like "Oh … I should be worried about this' and I am really worried about this and then I feel guilty for kind of almost wanting it … and then I just feel really fucked up so it would be nice to know definitively how, when it was gonna be because the uncertainty is like not good for my mental health, is what it comes down to basically.' (Carey)

They are experiencing a thought that if this terrible thing happened there is this way they could get around the waiting list, but that would be dangerous and scary in its own right and they feel guilty for even entertaining the idea. They also highlight again the issue of not knowing how long the queue is, that it is not only the waiting that is bad for their mental health but the not knowing how long the wait will be.

Participants' experiences of and attitudes toward waiting were not consistent but changed over time and with the situation. Ben, who waited two months to get on testosterone privately, a wait he described as quite quick, hated waiting the 20 minutes that his Testogel would take to dry each day so he switched to an injectable form of testosterone. This type of short-term waiting differs from the longer-term waiting where life continues through the waiting process. Barbara Adam sees this type of waiting as being more difficult because of the commodification of time in contemporary society:

> Today the idea that time is money is so deeply entrenched in the industrial way of life that no aspect of social existence is exempt from its practical expression. It is implicated when mothers rush to get the children dressed for school, when we opt for the fastest mode of transport, when we are obliged to wait in the doctor's surgery. (Adam, 2004: 127)

Wasting time is equated to wasting money, or at least to wasting something valuable, so the time it takes Ben's testosterone gel to dry is seen as wasted and therefore distressing in a way that waiting for the testosterone prescription while getting on with day to day life was not. Similarly, experiences of long-term waiting can change under different circumstances. Dan found that he initially thought he could wait for bottom surgery but that perspective changed. He explained:

> '[E]specially before my top surgery where I was just like, I think at the minute it's not my priority, I'll just wait until they can grow me my own penis in a little petri dish and I'll have it implanted it's fine I can wait. And then of course time goes on and you have the top surgery and it's like ah I don't know if I can wait.' (Dan)

Once he had hormones and top surgery, which for him were more urgent, his patience for bottom surgery dwindled.

Dan also described a difference between his understanding of what constitutes the waiting time and what the doctor at the GIC counted as waiting. This interaction happened when he had his second appointment at the GIC after going private for hormones and top surgery while on the waiting list. His GIC requires a minimum six-month wait from assessment to getting top surgery but Dan did things quicker by going private.

> 'First he told me that I had my chest surgery too soon and when I asked why and he said "Well we like to make sure that people are pretty sound on and they know and they're not gonna regret it" and I went "Well if I regretted it it wouldn't fall on you guys anyway it would fall on them" and the fact is I already waited you know even if we said from when I was an adult that's still 16 years to actually do any of this stuff.' (Dan)

For Dan, he has been waiting his entire adult life if not longer for these hormones and surgeries, he has been marking time outside of the system. The doctor only recognizes time marked in the system. Your waiting does not count until you enter the official queue. Emily describes her experience with a doctor at a different GIC who was also hyper-aware of the official queue. When I asked her if there was anything else that she was asking the GIC for that they were not willing to offer she replied:

> 'Facial surgery, and they just said it ain't, that ain't happening. And I said this to [the doctor] actually I'm prepared to be a test case and ... he was like "Oh we've already got test cases" and he just wanted me off the books because they're having a lot more people coming in ... who knows what happened to all those patients who fell at one of the hurdles on the way there you know where they're expected to wait for a year or they've got a GP that isn't helpful.' (Emily)

Her experience of waiting was not only at the beginning, waiting to access the system, but also waiting within the system for something she would never receive. Once they had determined her transition was finished, she was discharged to make room for the next person on the waiting list. She also recognizes that not everyone will make it on or through that waiting list.

What makes waiting easier?

Some waits are more difficult than others. Of course the length of the wait is a significant factor but there are other elements that can make the wait seem more or less difficult. From a non-healthcare perspective, business management expert David H. Maister lays out some of these factors as they are relevant to a modern, Western context in 'The Psychology of Waiting

Lines'. One of these principles is that people who are waiting 'want to get started' (Maister, 2005: 3). They want confirmation that they have not been forgotten, that it is known that they are waiting. We can see this with Carey's waiting for a letter saying 'welcome to the waiting list', they want official confirmation that the waiting process has started. This may also impact people's experience of waiting outside versus inside the system. The wait to get in the door might be more difficult in this way than all the subsequent waits for services once inside the GIC system. Another principle that has come up frequently is that 'uncertain waits are longer than known, finite waits' (Maister, 2005: 5). I found that participants were keeping abreast of the estimated GIC wait times and Carey specifically expressed that not knowing how long the wait was going to be made it worse, a sentiment I share. The Royal College of Psychiatrists has also recognized how distressing unknown waits can be. Their position is as follows:

> As a matter of good practice, service providers should take all reasonable steps to provide the patient with a realistic understanding of the time scales involved. Patients should have confidence that their treatment will progress in the agreed time scale. Service providers should also continually seek ways to help guarantee deadlines. (Royal College of Psychiatrists, 2013: 18)

Finally, Maister asserts that 'solo waits are longer than group waits' (2005: 8). While this sort of long-term waiting takes place in the background of one's day to day life, the communities that trans people create and seek out, such as the online support groups, can make the waiting process far less lonely.[9]

Taking time

In her 2017 article 'Taking (My) Time: Temporality in Transition, Queer Delays and Being (in the) Present', sociologist and trans activist Atalia Israeli-Nevo takes a different look at waiting. She uses autobiographical narrative to understand taking time as a method of creating trans identity in a way that is mindful and purposeful. She explains her experience as follows:

> Everywhere around me I felt enormous pressure either to forfeit this 'trans escapade,' or to 'go on with it.' The cis people around me were puzzled, anxious and sometimes angry with the fact that I demanded to be addressed with female pronouns and considered a woman without (at least seemingly) making any efforts to pass as a woman, except for wearing dresses and skirts. On the other hand, a lot of trans people were puzzled as well, and decided that the fact that I did not immediately choose to take hormones and pursue top and bottom surgery made

me genderqueer, and were sometimes baffled by the fact that I dared to call myself a transwoman. (Israeli-Nevo, 2017: 38)

She chooses to take her time with her transition, carefully considering each potential step and thus resisting expectations of passing and of a quick and linear transition path. With the current NHS wait times, this taking time could even occur while 'marking time in the system'. I was advised (and have advised others in turn) to get referred to the GIC as quickly as possible and figure out what interventions, if any, you want from them in the years you will be waiting anyway. This sort of efficient waiting is not necessarily in the spirit of 'taking one's time', but in a system where one could carefully consider their next step, come to a decision, and then have to wait years to access that step, it makes sense. Israeli-Nevo recognizes that taking this time is a privilege she has, that she is safer as a white woman whereas a trans woman of color may have to rush to pass for her own safety. There is also a class consideration here, that while she is choosing to take her time for other trans people that choice is made for them due to not being able to afford a speedy transition. However, as someone who is able to make that choice she finds taking her time to be a grounding experience, anchoring her in the present rather than in some longed for future.

> As trans subjects in this transphobic world, we are encouraged and forced into a position of not being present. We are dissociated from our bodies, our loved ones, and our general environment. This dissociation throws us into a far future in which we are safe after we have passed and found a bodily and social home. However, this future is imagined and unreachable, resulting in us being out of time. (Israeli-Nevo, 2017: 38)

Refusing to root one's life and one's transition in a future and instead taking one's time and staying in the present is a radical reclamation of time for the trans people who are able to do so.

Space

Waiting rooms

In contrast to the long-term waits to access services there are also short-term waits on the day of an appointment or procedure. This type of waiting has a unique arena, the waiting room. Emily described the waiting room as the physical manifestation of the waiting list, which helped her contextualize her being discharged.

> 'I remember when at that particular appointment and the one previous the waiting room was completely full you know I mean standing up.

There were no seats for people, everyone, you had people standing you know filling the space and it was like something's got to give. And yes they cleared their books of the ones that he considered to be less dysphoric and were coping in society, felt brutal obviously but hey.' (Emily)

She also detailed the atmosphere of that waiting room and other waiting rooms where groups of trans people wait for healthcare.

'I know that, that I could be waiting for an appointment at [the GIC] and instantly things could turn into a little social event with chatting and talking about experiences and things, but that was never encouraged you know cause it's a hospital waiting room. I mean it's obviously you know comfy chairs and all that but it's still a hospital waiting room. And when that started to happen that's how [the trans sexual health clinic] is … they encouraged it and they've got greeters now who where people are feeling like too nervous to join in where a greeter will sit and quietly talk to them one to one and then introduce them into a social atmosphere so some people come just to sit in reception there.' (Emily)

These spaces defy the expectation of a hospital waiting room. Where one might expect a quiet, staid atmosphere there is laughter and socializing. They are transformed into spaces to meet new friends, catch up with people you know, and offer and receive support from people going through a similar experience.

This contrasts with Flora's experience of getting private care. For them the lack of a concrete physical space was off-putting. For one they felt that not having the whole practice in one office impacted productivity.

'I don't know who the secretary is … but, they don't have offices. I think he probably goes to a cafe to do his, you know emails … also from [his] Twitter once I saw, they were in a pub and it was like "secretary meeting" or something and I was like right … so this is your business. Do you know what I mean like, so I just I on the one hand I'm sort of like it's humorous but then on the other hand I'm like so this is why you take forever to reply to my emails.' (Flora)

They also noted that the rented office space they went to for appointments lacked the specific identity and atmosphere that Emily described earlier, noting that "there are just random people in the waiting room" (Flora). In this type of more temporary and partial space an identity and sense of community is unable to take hold. This is especially true when there is no waiting room at all. Ben sought private healthcare through a remote service which he found to be quick and efficient but impersonal, remarking that "everything is kind of like done online so you're always talking to sort of a faceless person, you don't really know who they are". He, like Flora's experience with their private service, also noted that it could be difficult to get ahold of staff and that their phone line was often busy and he couldn't get through.

Anti-trans architecture

In *Transgender Architectonics: The Shape of Change in Modernist Space* Lucas Crawford discusses the ways in which transness and architecture are inherently related. Architecture is gendered (and gendering) and transness is spatial, they argue, 'space and self are never so distinct' (Crawford, 2015: 4). Space can help construct and support identity, but oftentimes architecture, or specific spaces, are in direct conflict with transness and trans people: 'trans women are routinely barred from crisis shelters; many of us lack of a place to properly eliminate waste in public; the public sphere itself is a series of architectures that sometimes seem designed to keep others vigilant in their surveillance of our bodies' (Crawford, 2015: 19). Feminist scholar Sally Munt experienced this as a lesbian living first in Brighton, which they describe as having 'constructed my lesbian identity', and later in Nottingham, which was hostile to them, particularly as a butch lesbian (1995: 115). Here space, understood on quite a large scale as entire cities, has the power to entirely construct, confirm, and support or to restrict and suppress a queer identity.

This ability of space to make or break identity can also be understood on a much (spatially) smaller scale. Bathrooms in particular are an obvious site of clashing between transness and physical space. To understand this clashing, Crawford explores the bathroom of the Brasserie restaurant designed by the firm DS+R. They argue throughout their book that a key gendered element to space is that architecture, structure, and exteriors are coded as masculine whereas décor and interiors are coded as feminine. Therefore, the latter is dismissed as frivolous and not respected the way that architecture or other forms of art are. As Crawford explains: 'The abjection of décor in modernist architecture finds a literal analogue in transgender's abjection from contemporary public washrooms: we are often regarded as figures of bodily excess or dishonest adornment ourselves' (2015: 47). In the realm of humanity, cis bodies are the architecture and a trans experience is the décor. Cis bodies are the necessary building blocks of the human experience and transness the frivolous décor of (assumed) bodily alterations and gendered expressions. In analyzing the particular space of the Brasserie, Crawford notes:

> DS+R have shown us precisely why washroom rhetoric and campaigns are so relevant and sensible at the current moment, at a time when

the fictional 'pure' functionality of unadorned architecture still passes as every bit as normal and harmless as the normative, straight, white, able, and middle-class male body passes as unadorned or unconstructed. (Crawford, 2015: 62, original emphasis)

Through understanding this connection between transness and architecture emerges a deeper understanding about how trans people and trans bodies are understood in society.

In addition to representing a broader framework of transness, bathrooms also play a crucial role in creating and maintaining gender. It is one of the very few places that adults, at least, are consistently segregated by gender in a Euro-American context. Thus it is a point of stress for many trans people and has become a legal battleground for the right for trans people to participate in public life. While often a difficult decision based on personal safety, choosing which bathroom to go into can be a radical pronouncement of one's identity and everyone in that restroom is participating in either reifying or rejecting the gendered assertions of the other occupants. One participant, George, echoes this when he talks about how accepting the school he works in has been of his gender identity in exactly these terms; he quotes his boss as saying, "Okay you can only take the boys to the toilet and you can use the men's toilet and you are a man." This practice adds to the 'gender archive', 'we are not observers or pre-gendered visitors to washrooms; we too are archives of gender affect, and each washroom we visit becomes a part of that archive' (Crawford, 2015: 63). These visits to the bathroom, whether challenged or unchallenged, make up the gender experience of any visitor, trans or cis.

I see this idea of interactions with certain spaces as gender archival practice as logically extending to the more purposeful acts of doing gender; interactions with the GIC, GP surgery, hospitals, pharmacies, and so on. By merely showing up to these places in the capacity that a trans person does, seeking transition related healthcare, is not only adding to the archive of that person's gender identity but of their gender history. When Adam describes himself as a man with a "trans history", he is explaining that not only has his gender been archived and continues to be archived as male, but that this archive has been/is being curated in a certain way, in a trans way. The difference between Adam and a cis man then is not gender identity, but how they have archived their gender. Adam has taken extra steps that a cis man would not have to take, going to his GP to get a referral, visiting the GIC, navigating through the offices of the different gatekeepers at the GIC, continuing to go to the pharmacy to obtain his testosterone and estrogen blockers, going to a walk-in once a month to have his estrogen blockers administered, and eventually going to hospitals to have transition related surgeries. All of this is part of the process of archiving transness, of archiving not just gender but trans gender.

My experience of going into public restrooms is a consistently fraught part of curating my gender archive. Going into a gender-neutral restroom is thrilling precisely because it is an experience that aligns with my existing gender archive in addition to the relief of feeling safe there. When no such restroom is available and I have to choose between a men's or a women's space, there is tension. Should I abandon the carefully curated project of archiving a comfortably masculine gender to go into the women's restroom where I will likely be safer? In that space I am sometimes (much less so after top surgery) affirmed by the other participants but rejected by myself. In the men's restroom I am often (although certainly not always) rejected by the other participants but experience less cognitive dissonance with my existing gender archive. The purposeful acts of gender archive have, for me, been a much more positive experience. Going to my GP to get a referral to the GIC was a thoroughly affirming experience in which the two of us both contributed to my (trans)gender archive. I reified my non-binary gender and trans history by making and showing up to that appointment and going through the hoops of accessing a referral. My GP made unique contributions to my gender archive by not knowing 'which way I was going' (basically they did not know if I was assigned female at birth or assigned male at birth), which affirmed that I am seen as at least somewhat gender non-conforming. By posing the questions on the form to me they also caused me to decide on a narrative of my gender that I will use to access transition related healthcare. This experience at my GPs, while a frustrating interaction with bureaucracy, also contributed positively to my (trans)gender archive both in reifying my non-binary gender but also because I have now experienced something which many other trans people have had to experience, reifying my trans history.

Axes of power

What all of these elements have in common is that they enact power over trans people in a way that can jeopardize their health. With the complex medical bureaucracy there are many hurdles at which someone could fall before seeking transition related healthcare. In addition to that bureaucracy, other state bureaucracies (such as marriage or obtaining a Gender Recognition Certificate) are damaging in the way they take power for gender identification away from trans people and consistently erase gender diversity. Time is manipulated with inordinately long wait times for gender services in the NHS, although some people take that power back by choosing to take their time and/or by paying to go private and shorten their wait time if they are able to. There are also spaces, notably bathrooms, which can be fraught for trans people to exist in but also a reclamation of space in the way trans waiting rooms are constructed by their inhabitants. Throughout this chapter it is clear that the story of trans health in the UK is not as simple as one of succumbing to the whims of powerful state and medical entities. This understanding of how trans people are subsumed under these power structures is continuously challenged by the ways in which they resist and overcome the barriers these structures put in place. These strategies for overcoming barriers are addressed in the following final chapter.

6

Pedagogy and TransLiteracy

'Like everybody's on YouTube and everybody's trans.'

Ben

In this chapter I respond to the previous two chapters outlining barriers to trans health by discussing how those barriers are sometimes overcome.[1] This chapter is largely descriptive of a specific moment in time and space,[2] but this description is valuable in answering in understanding, when they are able to at all, how trans people overcome barriers to accessing quality healthcare. Firstly, I identify what trans people need to learn in order to access quality healthcare within a system ill-equipped to serve them. I especially highlight the strategic use of personal narrative but there are a myriad of things that make up these trans specific knowledges, the amalgamation of which I call TransLiteracy. Secondly, I look at how trans knowledges are disseminated and what makes this dissemination effective. I understand this system of distributing knowledge as a form of pedagogy, one that is not based in any particular institution but is rather a tool used widely by trans communities to improve health outcomes. The two key features of this type of pedagogy that I identify are that it is decentralized and social. Both aspects are important in ensuring that helpful information is disseminated broadly, and contextualized, which can improve trans health through increasing access to quality healthcare and through building social bonds. This discussion supports previous work by Israeli-Nevo, Spade, Ponse, Pearce, Raun, Andrews, Zhao et al, and Duguay and extends that of Latham and Poster.

Pedagogy

Many trans people become quite adept at educating themselves, care providers, and others within their communities. When accessing healthcare, trans people learn to deploy personal narrative as well as being prepared to educate medical care providers and gatekeepers on medical practice and policy. In order for this education to take place the trans person must first acquire the knowledge themselves, which in turn requires them to know where and how to look for such knowledge. This education happens through community relationships which help trans people learn to advocate for themselves in healthcare and other settings. Currently a large portion of this education takes place online, so the social internet[3] plays a crucial role in the building of these communities and the dissemination of this knowledge. These social and decentralized methods of knowledge sharing form an alternative model of pedagogy within trans communities, one that is crucial for trans people seeking to access quality healthcare.

The material: TransLiteracy

There are certain things trans people have to know and skills they must acquire in order to navigate their healthcare and the wider world. Based on my own experience seeking this information, existing in trans communities where this information is being requested and/or shared, and the literature and experiences of the participants I will outline in the sections that follow, there are several important categories of knowledge. For altering gender presentation people may seek help on ways to cut and style hair, how to tuck, pack, or pad, safe binding practices, how to apply makeup, and advice on styles and brands of clothing. When looking into surgical options they may ask for pictures of people's results as well as guidance on which surgeries and surgical methods to seek out, which surgeons and hospitals are best for what they want, how to get time off work, how to get funding for these procedures, help quitting smoking or losing weight to prepare for surgery, tips for healing, and how to minimize or cover surgery scars. If they are just starting to come out and socially transition, trans people may look for advice on coming out in different areas of their life such as to parents, siblings, extended family, work, school, partners, children, and so on, specifically regarding things like what to say, when the best time is to do it, and what to do if the person or institution reacts negatively. They may also require information about how to legally change their name, how to change their gender marker and get new government documents, and how to navigate various bureaucracies including the process for obtaining a Gender Recognition Certificate. If they are considering hormones they might want to know what changes they can expect from hormones and in what timeframe they can expect those changes, the benefits and challenges of different hormone delivery options, how to get blood work done, how to read the blood work results, what healthy hormone levels are, and even connections to buy hormones or injecting supplies. In terms of more generally accessing transition related healthcare this would include knowing the respective wait times for different gender identity clinics (GICs) and/or private providers as well as other factors to help choose the best one to be referred to, the benefits and drawbacks of going private versus going through the National Health Service (NHS), how to find which General Practitioner (GP)/surgery in the area will give a referral to the GIC, how to approach and in some cases convince the GP to give a GIC referral, coping mechanisms to employ during long wait times, how to access funding, what is on offer from the GICs or private providers, and how to deploy personal narrative to get certain things from a given provider. This knowledge also extends to general NHS policies, for example, both Adam and Dan referenced the policy of an 18-week minimum wait for specialist services.

With healthcare that is not explicitly transition related, questions could be about how to maintain fertility, what health screenings are needed for different bodies, how to access those screenings, and tips for looking after mental health and seeking therapy or other mental health services. This extensive list is merely scratching the surface. For every one of the many ways a trans person's life is complicated by their transness, for every healthcare interaction they have, and for every healthcare decision they have to make, there is a resource of trans people who have either gone before and can thus offer their advice based on personal experience or at the very least can provide support and solidarity. This resource can be accessed in numerous ways which I will discuss in this chapter. This is not to say that personal experience is the only mode of knowledge valued: classifications of expertise that are important in the offline world are certainly recreated in these online spaces. For example, when someone asks a legal question in one of the online support groups I belong to, members always tag the lawyers in the group who can in some cases give both their personal experience and professional legal expertise. In this case, having a diversity of experiences both as trans people and as experts in other fields increases the knowledges available to teach and learn. This collective community experience forms the curriculum and participants can alternately act as the educator or knowledge distributor and as the student or knowledge seeker.

Deploying personal narrative

Of all the information and skills listed here, perhaps the most important aspect of TransLiteracy that people learn through this alternative pedagogy is how to construct a personal narrative. In her piece 'Taking (My) Time: Temporality in Transition, Queer Delays and Being (in the) Present', Atalia Israeli-Nevo discusses constructing trans time through narrative. In '[examining] the practice of being/making/creating/developing trans identity through the notion of "taking one's time"', she challenges pre-existing narratives that call for an instantaneous, or at least quick, transition (2017: 35). She consciously took her time developing her trans identity and thus time itself became a part of her narrative. In this way narrative can be a site where trans people reclaim agency and resist a more limited definition of trans experience. Narrative can also be crucial for creating a positive interaction with medical systems, where both patients and medical professionals (co)construct narratives that connect the dots between the person the patient was/is before, the medical crisis or encounter, and the person they are/will become (see Mattingly [1994] on therapeutic emplotment and Huss-Ashmore [2000] on therapeutic narrative). Collaborating to produce these narratives are some of the sites of intra-action that I outlined in Chapter 3. Furthermore, the act of constructing this narrative can contribute to one's gender archive, as I discussed in Chapter 5.

Penis = ?

When speaking about transmasculine people, J.R. Latham (2016) unpacks how male as a sex is created and understood through narrative. Trans men are frequently challenging heteronormative narratives such as the idea that they should only be attracted to cis women, that they should have no sex before bottom surgery, that they should enjoy sex after surgery, and even that they should have bottom surgery at all. When understanding the trans penis (or your own penis as a trans person), Latham explains that language is crucial and is constructed in relation to the self and in collaboration with sexual partners, thus 'materialising a "male sex organ" via translating one object into another, both narratively and practically' (2016: 148). I understand this through the equation penis = phallus + narrative.[4] In this equation, a penis could be the result of phalloplasty or metoidioplasty, what is usually referred to as a clitoris, a strap-on, a packer, et cetera (phallus + narrative) and what is usually referred to as a penis need not actually be a penis (phallus - narrative).[5] Only some of these narrative constructions require the collaboration of medical care providers. This narrative construction can also be used in conjunction with incorporealating and disincorporealating practices (such as packing and tucking), as I highlighted in Chapter 3.

Accessing care

While narrative can be used more personally, as in the case of phallus +/- narrative, to benefit the construction of the self, many trans people must also learn how to deploy personal narrative to access care and services. For example, Ben, who presented a carefully constructed narrative in order to access transition related healthcare:

> 'I lied to be honest, I completely lied and just said all of the things that I knew they wanted me to say and then that's how I did it because I knew that I wanted testosterone and that was the most effective way to get testosterone. If I was gonna start telling the truth about every little thing that's gonna be more of a block so I just kind of went for what I wanted. … I left a lot of stuff rather than actually lie, but left out the part that my dad is not supportive because one of my friends

was held back quite a lot because his parents weren't supportive. They wanted to get like all of this information about his parents and stuff even though he was over 18 … and then I omitted pretty much everything about being sort of non-binary or anything like that. I didn't want to give them the impression that I was like wishy-washy, not that that's what that is but I think that's what people think that it is you know? So I just pretended that I just 100 per cent knew from when I was like one or something.' (Ben)

When presenting to a GP, GIC, or private gender specialist in order to access transition related healthcare trans people have learned what care providers are looking for, or what boxes they have to tick as was discussed in the previous chapter. This is part of what Dean Spade calls 'the long-standing practice amongst gender variant people of strategically deploying medically-approved narratives in order to obtain body-alteration goals' (2000/2006: 16). Spade harkens back to the story of Agnes who in 1958 presented to doctors in Los Angeles as an intersex person who had female secondary sexual characteristics but a penis and scrotum which were removed with surgery. Agnes later revealed that those female secondary sexual characteristics had been the result of self-medicating with estrogen since age 12 and not an intersex variation. In the UK in the 1950s Roberta Cowell presented similarly to doctors as intersex in order to access treatment.[6] At that time the only way to access transition related healthcare was if the bodily changes were presented as fixing a biological 'condition' rather than fulfilling the patient's desire for a bodily alteration.

While trans people no longer have to present as intersex to access hormones and surgeries, there are still medical understandings of what a trans person is that they can choose to either align themselves with or to reject at the risk of not being able to access the care they are seeking. When the first gender clinics in the US started seeing patients they were using Harry Benjamin's 1966 book *The Transsexual Phenomenon* as a reference for how to diagnose and treat trans people. They found that the patients at their clinics matched up perfectly with Benjamin's criteria:

> [I]t took a surprisingly long time – several years – for the researchers to realize that the reason the candidates' behavioral profiles matched Benjamin's so well was that the candidates, too, had read Benjamin's book, which was passed from hand to hand within the transsexual community, and they were only too happy to provide the behavior that led to acceptance for surgery. (Stone, 1991/2006: 228)

Before the internet these peer networks shared knowledge on how to access surgery by learning the criteria from the same source the medical care providers were and showing them what they expected to see. However, Spade problematizes the idea that trans people are 'only too happy' to conform to expectations to access care. They note:

> Personal narrative is always strategically employed. It is always mediated through cultural understandings, through ideology. It is always a function of selective memory and narration. Have I learned that I should lie to obtain surgery, as others have before me? Does that lesson require an acceptance that I cannot successfully advocate on behalf of a different approach to my desire for transformation? (Spade, 2000/2006: 328)

Spade has learned how to strategically craft and deploy narrative to access care but they are questioning whether or not they want to use that knowledge or if they would rather challenge those assumptions and advocate for themselves in another way.

These conversations continue to happen within trans communities, including advice on how to access non-binary and non-linear transitions, but today they are primarily happening online, as I will discuss in the following sections.

Finding community

While they are not foolproof, there are certain ways trans people have of recognizing fellow trans people in public which can be useful for embarking on community building. Barbara Ponse found that this was the case with closeted lesbians in the 1970s being able to identify each other without outing themselves: 'A standard feature of gay lore is that "it takes one to know one." It seems that this is not attributable to any mystical sixth sense but rather to a sensitivity-honed by the experience of passing-to the subtleties of various cues' (1976: 320). The specific things they were picking up on included:

> The failure to say certain things—for example, to specify the gender of an individual referred to in a conversation—to be secretive about one's personal life, to express a lack of interest in males, to never having been married, to have a roommate, and to fail to present a male companion at appropriate times can start the speculative ball rolling on the part of a gay woman that another woman may, indeed, herself be gay. (Ponse, 1976: 320)

Ponse found that once these lesbians had a hunch that someone was gay, they would tread carefully, testing their hypothesis. They would do this by 'dropping pins', or mentioning things that would have special meaning to a gay person and judging their reaction. Additionally, '[a]n audience to whom a gay identity is to be revealed might be sounded about their attitudes toward gay people or toward minorities in general' (Ponse, 1976: 331). These strategies allowed the women to not out themselves directly and could happen in front of straight people without them realizing.

In the case of trans people, if someone uses certain terminology, is wearing certain articles such as a pronoun badge or something with the trans flag, or reveals certain details about their life it can indicate to someone else in the know that this person may also be trans. All of these signals can be given in online spaces as well, such as through the terminology used and details shared in posted content, listing pronouns in profiles, and posting or sharing trans related images or content. I personally frequently wear a pronoun badge, am openly trans in my social media profiles, and disclose that I am trans to other people in the hope that they feel comfortable disclosing to me and we can connect. In any public situation, it can be comforting and feel safer to identify if there is another trans person around. In social situations, identifying other trans people is how you build community or get connected with existing communities of similar people, which is positive for people's mental health and allows for the kind of education that helps them access healthcare.

Trans dialect

An important facet in community building is having a shared language. Within the English speaking population in the UK that I am a part of and conducted research with, trans people have a shorthand consisting of abbreviations and slang terms that allow us to quickly, easily, and sometimes covertly, communicate with each other.[7] This language is learned through the same online and offline methods as healthcare knowledge. It consists of a literacy around discussing gender and a shorthand for celebrating, connecting, educating, and grieving. One celebratory example is people marking alternate 'birthdays'. For some people this birthday is the day they came out as trans, for some it is the day they started hormones, and for others this is the day that they had an important surgery or the last procedure they will be seeking for their transition. This is significant because the person is raising the importance of these moments in their gender history to the level of the day they came into existence. In some cases it is replacing that day, as if to say 'this is the day I was really born'. If they are celebrating starting testosterone, one might refer to this as their 'T-day'. While this is not explicitly using the language of birthdays, it mirrors the common abbreviation of 'B-day' for birthday, so saying something like 'happy T-day' evokes a similar type of celebration. Here people are explicitly bringing attention to the fact that it is an alternate birthday by saying 'happy T-day' rather than simple 'happy birthday', but that is not necessarily always the case.

Preparing for the worst

Much of what constitutes TransLiteracy, and indeed a significant portion of this book, focuses on negative experiences and 'worst-case scenarios'. In *Understanding Trans Health: Discourse, Power and Possibility*, Ruth Pearce discusses how this negativity operates, particularly when information is distributed online. She admits that '[the] discourse of difficulty perpetuates fear and concern amongst patients early in the transition process' but that the upside of this is that it 'also enables them to prepare' (2018: 144). Stories of mistreatment in healthcare services generally and gender services specifically can be scary, particularly for someone just beginning to understand their relationship to gender and/or without a strong trans network. Ben demonstrated this in our conversation when he commented, "when you're dealing with lots of different healthcare people you have to be careful where you tread, you don't know who's good and who's not so you have to kind of err on the side of caution really".

Carey described a similar feeling as well:

> '[W]hen I've been doing kind of research and reading about other people's experiences you know it might be that for every ten experiences that are good there's one experience that's bad but the bad one is gonna stick out more so I'm gonna be like "Oh one person four years ago had a bad experience trying to access gender treatment in Wales, it's gonna be terrible".' (Carey)

Ingrid completely avoided the GIC system because of the negative experiences of others:

> 'I didn't want to go through [the GIC] unless I absolutely had to you know. I knew a couple of other girls who had been through them and they kept talking about how badly they'd been bullied by the staff there, and because I was, you know, reasonably well off I thought "Well let's go private".' (Ingrid)

In Ingrid's case these experiences were directly from people she knows but Carey's research was mostly done online where stories are often undated and can be presented as current possibilities even if they occurred in the past. When things improve, some of these 'horror stories' may no longer be likely to occur. However, there is certainly still transphobia throughout healthcare systems which cannot and should not be ignored. Strategically deploying mistrust, much like deploying personal narrative, can make for more adept patients. As Pearce says: 'I know that transphobia and cisgenderism are common; some level of mistrust *feels* like a rational, strategic response that enables me to manage my expectations for the future and reduce uncertainty' (2018: 154, original emphasis).

So, in many ways, the material here that makes up TransLiteracy is readying trans people for all of the difficulties and complexities that have been described in the previous chapters. It is shrewdly preparing them for the worst so that at least they are not surprised by barriers to good health and quality healthcare when they encounter them, and hopefully it is helping them to overcome those barriers that do arise.

The methods
Social media

Like many other marginalized groups, trans people have turned to online spaces in order to build communities and exchange information (Mehra et al, 2006). As Pearce explains, '[the] internet provided a vital catalyst for the trans social movement to grow and change, as a formerly largely invisible and geographically dispersed population was empowered to come together and organise on an unprecedented scale' (Pearce, 2018: 39). These spaces are frequently focused on community education where members can be alternately student and teacher. Some individuals may be valued more highly as educators due to their level of experience, for example someone who has been out and navigating the healthcare system for 20 years will have a wealth of knowledge to share with people who have only come out more recently. This can be seen in spaces such as Facebook groups where there will be a few more experienced members who are the most frequent commenters and may act as group moderators as well as on YouTube where a single channel may only have one or a few educators speaking to many more viewers. However, within each platform as a whole the fact that anyone with the resources to do so can comment on a Facebook post or upload a video makes the knowledge production and dispersal decentralized.

Media studies scholar Mark Poster noted in their 1995 paper 'Postmodern Virtualities' that it was the telephone rather than the television or the radio that was the most radical new communication form during the first media age precisely because it is decentralized. Anyone with a phone can be the message sender or the message receiver and people switch between roles in different times and in different exchanges. The traditional barriers to who gets to construct a message to be broadcast are eliminated when the majority of people can pick up a phone and relay their message to any individual they can call. In the modern media age this is echoed and amplified by the internet, particularly the social internet. As Poster sees it, the internet 'combines the decentralized model of the telephone and its numerous "producers" of messages with the broadcast model's advantage of numerous receivers' (1995: 91). It is this decentralized model that allows for trans people (and other marginalized people) who do not have easy access to broadcasting their message through mainstream media to tell their stories. The internet in general and the social internet specifically are uniquely friendly to transness. Certainly not in the sense of using the internet as a trans person, which is often rife with harassment,[8] but rather the structure of the internet independent of its users. The internet queers temporality; it is an archive where old and new content co-mingle and nothing is finite. The internet is fluid and changeable, content can be deleted and edited, autobiographies are continuously updated, communities emerge, change, and die out. It allows for multiplicity of identity; one can have multiple profiles on a single platform, multiple profiles across multiple platforms, all of which can have a unique personality, tone, aesthetic, identity, and audience. In this way it is no surprise that the internet has emerged as a key place where trans people can go to better understand their relationship with gender, to find and build communities, and participate in the information exchanges that develop TransLiteracy. Specifically, as it is relevant to this work, the internet more broadly and social media in particular are places trans people go to seek and share information about health and healthcare.

YouTube and vlogging

With the advent of the video sharing platform YouTube in 2005 and its subsequent rise in popularity, creating video content and reaching an audience became more widely accessible. This has become an important avenue for trans people to find information, especially young trans people and/or those just beginning to understand their gender identity. In my years of watching trans YouTube content I've come across videos discussing different facets of identity, tips for altering gender presentation, advice on coming out, records of changes from taking hormones, experiences of different surgeries, tips on accessing healthcare and navigating bureaucracies, and so on. The first-hand experiences of other trans people can be invaluable, particularly if someone does not know any trans people in 'real life'.

YouTube was absolutely crucial for me as a young queer person. I did not see positive trans role models in the media and I did not know any openly trans people personally so I sought out videos from people who would talk about their identity and document their transition. This pursuit gave words to the feelings I was experiencing, provided a sense of hope that I could one day be myself, and introduced me to a community I belonged in, all of which were beneficial to my mental health. Adam also found YouTube videos helpful in understanding his identity, he recalled identifying with vlogs and blog posts by trans people as well as a YouTube series created by a non-binary therapist which answered a lot of questions he had while coming to terms with being trans and starting his transition. He even recalled being surprised when he related to a specific YouTuber:

> 'I didn't think that this is where I would identify as strongly but it's amazing that I do, I find a lot of the time that I actually identify with Kat Blaque[9] ... when she refers to her transness because ... I was watching a video yesterday ... and what she said was "I think of myself as a woman with a trans history" and I immediately was like there it is.' (Adam)

Despite Adam having a different gender experience than Blaque, when he heard this specific way of describing transness he could immediately relate to it. He now uses that phraseology to refer to himself, describing himself as a man with a trans history. It is also interesting that he was watching this video the day before we spoke. Although he was no longer at the early stages of understanding his gender identity and was already on testosterone, he was still consuming content by and learning from trans YouTubers. Similarly when another participant, Dan, was describing an experience he was currently dealing with he said, "I remember watching, I think a YouTuber that said your dysphoria just kind of shifts and you don't lose it." He had gotten the words to explain his experiences and confirmation that his experiences were normal from a YouTube video, even as someone who was already comfortable in his gender identity and had made significant progress toward his transition goals. Another participant, Holly, also mentioned watching YouTube videos, a comment that caused her to break out in laughter. She went on to elaborate that as an older person it helped her to hear some perspectives from younger people. She herself made a YouTube video to come out as HIV+, another part of her experience that she felt was important to speak about openly and publicly.

Where Adam, Dan, and Holly benefited from watching these videos, Ben lamented that when he was young the selection of trans YouTube videos was not as large and varied as it is today:

> 'You know like I remember looking for videos when I was like 17–18 and there was like three or four people and they were all really far along the line so you didn't really relate and you didn't really understand what was happening you know. But now it's all over the place so I feel like I'd be a lot better off.' (Ben)

For him, not having content that showed people at the beginning stages of understanding and realizing their identity made it difficult to relate to the content. He feels that were he coming to terms with his identity today he would have benefited greatly from the content currently available on the platform. This highlights the importance of having a diversity of representation on places like YouTube, not just in the sense that trans content is available but that the trans content is itself diverse. This means representing a variety of identities under the trans umbrella as well as different experiences, transition goals, races, ages, and so on.

The importance of these trans related vlogs is not just the impact for the viewer but what the process means for the person making the videos. Even in the very early stages of the internet, Mark Poster remarked that 'the appeal is strong to tell one's tale to others, to many, many others' (1995: 91). This drive to tell one's story is strong within trans communities and for many the act of discussing their gender identity and experiences as a trans person, documenting the process of their transition, and engaging with an audience are a crucial part of the way they enact their transness. As communications and trans studies scholar Tobias Raun puts it, vlogs:

> engender the ongoing process of 'becoming' man/woman/trans by (re)learning, testing, evaluating in front of the camera the act of gender. This includes using the vlog as an extended mirror, inscribing the vlogger in multiple and intersubjective reflections, being visible to themselves and others as an image – an image that they can engage with and/or that others can support and confirm. (Raun, 2016: 376)

Being out as trans on the internet is a declaration far more public that can reach far more people than most individuals are capable of doing offline. The act of making this public declaration helps cement a self-awareness of one's (trans)gender identity while simultaneously allowing for experimentation and growth. It is also through this process that both the video creator and the viewers are learning and developing the skill of crafting an autobiographical narrative, something they will need to deploy to access healthcare.

The role of the supportive audience in this relationship is to encourage and confirm. By engaging with other trans people or with cis allies on these social media platforms people have their gender affirmed and receive encouragement to continue moving forward. There are of course also unsupportive audiences who misgender, deadname,[10] and otherwise harass that trans people have to deal with. Despite the nature of the YouTube platform putting the power in the hands of the creator to decide how they want to present themselves, their message is not always decoded in the way they would hope. Much like with constructing a body image (Chapter 3) and a gendered archive (Chapter 5), some people will actively reject and resist what the trans person is trying to create. As art theorist and philosopher Jorella Andrews says in *Showing Off! A Philosophy of Image*:

> [T]o be a focus for attention, does not mean that you will be seen or heard on your own terms. There are other conditions of perception

and reception at issue, including the fact that relationships between expression and reception, between self-showing and being seen, can never be guaranteed to be reciprocal no matter how apparently unmediated they might be. (Andrews, 2014: 54)

This comes into play on trans YouTube when you have people who, for example, will always see a trans woman as a man no matter how much she explains and defends her womanhood, or people who cannot accept the existence of non-binary genders. No matter how much control a platform offers a content creator, they can never fully control how any individual viewer or the audience as a whole will perceive them.

From the perspective of the viewer of a YouTube video, the specific format of the platform is part of what makes it so uniquely valuable; particularly the fact that YouTube is a video medium and that public videos can be searched for and found by anyone. The combination of visual and auditory elements in a video medium are specifically useful for documenting transition.[11] For viewers who are accessing the visual content of the videos, vloggers can show outfits, demonstrate hair, makeup, and grooming techniques, and detail physical changes from hormones and/or surgery. For viewers accessing the audio content of the videos, vloggers can document vocal changes from hormones or surgery. The combination of the visual and the auditory along with the common blog format of one person speaking directly to the camera makes these videos seem personal. They are relatable because of their content but also because they give the impression of talking one-on-one with a friend. The public nature of YouTube and the fact that videos can be found by searching for key words is also important as it improves access. People do not need to belong to a group, have any connections with trans communities, or have come out in any way. Ben and I both turned to YouTube early on in the process of understanding our gender for this very reason. Anyone with unrestricted[12] internet access who is curious about gender diversity can go on YouTube and view content made by trans people. This in addition to the value of the first-hand knowledge and experience being shared makes it a great resource for people in the early stages of understanding their gender identity. It gave me the language to comprehend the way I was feeling and showed me non-cis possibilities for being in the world. The fact that you can search by specific topic (such as 'facial feminization surgery' or 'two years on testosterone') and the way that many vlogs document someone's experience over a length of time and through different points in their transition also makes it valuable for people at all different stages of their trans experience. Even someone who has been out for many years and has achieved some of their transition goals may turn to YouTube for information about the next surgery they want, for non-transition related advice, or just to watch someone they can relate to. The act of creating videos can also be a crucial part of being trans, helping people negotiate gender and build community. There is no discussing contemporary trans communities in the UK without discussing trans YouTube.

Facebook

While it is important to have this content openly available, it is also valuable to have spaces that are more private. Some trans people, such as those who are not yet out or who are stealth, may not feel comfortable participating in trans YouTube spaces precisely because they are so easily accessible. Others who are not concerned about people knowing they are trans may not want to discuss specific problems or ask 'embarrassing' questions in such a public forum. This is where other platforms come in. While YouTube is traditionally more open and public,[13] Facebook offers opportunities for more private discussions. Within an individual's page they can choose from a range of privacy settings to curate who sees any of their posts. This way someone could, for example, prevent certain family members from seeing their coming out post or limit a post about a specifically trans experience to a select group of Facebook friends. There are also many closed and secret[14] Facebook groups dedicated to trans people and different subgroups of trans people. In such groups it is possible to limit who can post, view posts, and comment to only people belonging to the relevant group.[15] Group membership can be further specified by career field or place of work, hobbies and interests, or specific experiences. Dan found this when he was researching bottom surgery options, "with abdominal phalloplasty … there's loads of different secret groups that you can go to on Facebook and they give you a little bit more information". He found that joining a group that is only for people who have had abdominal phalloplasty or who are considering that specific procedure he was able to get the first-hand experiences and information that helped him decide that that was the right surgery for him. This first-hand information is only available in this format because people who may not feel comfortable sharing intimate details about and even pictures of their genitals in a more public forum feel they can do so in this more private space as well as because this type of content would be flagged or removed from many more public platforms including if it was shared on a public Facebook group or profile.

 I have belonged to a number of trans Facebook groups over the years which I have used to get information about many of the topics I outlined at the beginning of the chapter. In one Facebook support network I am a part of I have posted seeking advice on how to deal with people's transphobic reactions when they find out the topic of my work, looking for inspiration as to what gender-neutral parent name my future kids could call me, asking what to bring to the appointment with my GP when I was asking for my referral to the GIC, celebrating getting my GIC referral while seeing if anyone had any advice for what to expect from the waiting process, looking for recommendations for masculine dress shirts that would fit my narrow shoulders, excitedly sharing that I had become an uncle with people I know wouldn't balk at my use of the masculine term, looking for a lead on a trans-friendly GP in the new area I moved to, other positive moments of gender euphoria,[16] and jokes that would only be funny to fellow trans people. Some of these were instances of directly seeking advice or information about accessing healthcare but all of them were positive for my mental health. Each question I asked was met with many helpful answers and every post with words of support. I have also had many opportunities to comment on other people's posts and offer my experience, assistance, or words of encouragement.[17] Along the way I am continuously learning how to navigate the NHS and the world as a trans person along with the knowledge that I am not alone in this experience.

Facebook can also serve another purpose, it can be instrumental in someone's coming out process. As you can have your name, gender, and a picture of yourself as part of your Facebook profile, it can be somewhat fraught for someone in the early stages of coming out as trans. I recall the day I changed my gender and pronouns on Facebook as a pivotal moment in my coming out. It was the first time I was publicly declaring my transness as I had previously only talked about my gender one-on-one with close friends. Updating my profile picture to one with a more masculine presentation was also important. Adam had a similar experience, but as he was changing his name as well and did not want to have to deal with untagging and deleting old pictures where he looked more feminine, he took a slightly different approach:

> 'When it came to my Facebook, my social media, I sort of actively created a completely new Facebook and deleted the old one and added the people that had known, that I had had those conversations with, to that new Facebook. And then it, I think other people maybe that I wasn't as close with saw the new Facebook profile with a new name attached and saw in the picture that it was me and so asked people that they saw who were mutual friends with me what the deal was with that and then those people acted as proxies.' (Adam)

For Adam, Facebook was a tool he used to help him come out. He made an entirely new account so he could have a fresh start and initially only added the close family and friends that he had already come out to. Then when he started showing up as a suggested friend on other people's Facebooks he gave his friends who already knew his gender history permission to come out for him, saving him from having to have as many coming out conversations as he otherwise would have. Others keep their same profile, simply changing the name and/or profile picture, sometimes coming out to their friends in a Facebook post.

In this way, Facebook is acting not only as a way for trans people to educate and learn from each other but also as a platform for trans people to educate their broader social network. This can certainly take the form of trans people sharing articles, linking to websites, or creating their own posts about trans issues in order to educate their friends and family. However, the type of education I am discussing here is trans people educating their Facebook friends about themselves. This can occur through the use of explicit and implicit identity statements, where 'explicit identity statements often take the form of autobiographic descriptions given by the users' and 'implicit identity statements can be found in the impressions "given off" by the users' (Zhao et al, 2008: 1820). An explicit identity statement in this example could be a formal coming out post where the person explains their gender along with things like the story of how they came to understand their gender, unveiling a new name, and/or declaring new pronouns. When looking at disclosure on social media of LGBTQ identity among young people, media and communications scholar Stefanie Duguay found that Facebook, specifically as opposed to Twitter, was seen as a reflection of your personal identity.

> With the platform's large volume of content, participants stated that LGBTQ-related messages also seemed subtler on Twitter and that it was a more appropriate space than Facebook for this subject matter. Holly, who does not express her lesbian identity on Facebook but frequently tweets about LGBTQ topics, affirmed that Twitter 'is more political generally as a medium … If someone saw something on here then they'd be more likely to think that it was just a political statement rather than actually sort of who you are'. (Duguay, 2016: 901)

Posting queer content on Facebook was avoided by these participants for precisely the same reason others choose to post there, because a post on Facebook is seen as an identity statement. Such a statement can be posted publicly, for Facebook friends only, for a specifically curated subset of Facebook friends, or can be slightly more private. For example, while I never made a dedicated coming out post on my public Facebook profile, I officially came out to my siblings over Facebook messenger a few years ago. This is the very definition of an explicit identity statement and is useful in getting important information about one's identity across quickly and clearly. Zhao et al found, however, that implicit identity statements were more common on Facebook. For trans people this can mean changing their profile picture to one where they have a certain gender presentation, changing their pronouns, posting photos of themselves at trans events, and so on. These two avenues of proclaiming identity on Facebook are an important part of the process of understanding, constructing, and publicizing one's relationship to gender.

Other social media platforms

Some participants discussed finding information beyond YouTube and Facebook, such as Emily who was previously active in now defunct Yahoo group or Carey who found a blog particularly helpful:

> 'I know another, well I don't know I follow their blog, another non-binary person in Wales who has just had top surgery without going on hormones so I know that that is a thing cause I was, most of the information out there is like you go to your appointment and then you go on hormones and then like a couple of years down the line then we'll see about whether you can have surgery or not. But because I don't think I wanna go down the hormones route I was like "Ah oh my god does that mean that I'm never gonna be able to have surgery unless I go on testosterone?" And then I found other people who are like "No, you don't have to change your body in ways that you don't want it to change you can change it in the ways that you do want it to change" and that was reassuring.' (Carey)

Carey was able to find someone they could identify with who had accessed the things they hope to access, assuring them that their transition goals are possible. Instagram is another outlet that did not come up as frequently in interviews but certainly has a strong trans presence. I personally follow trans friends, trans celebrities, accounts that repost or post submitted pictures of trans people, and the accounts of trans owned businesses. When Holly was struggling with her identity, she also found solace on Instagram:

> 'I went online, so I started seeing a lot of uh YouTube videos. A lot of that and I became friends with people online, Instagram mainly, that's what start changing my perspective. To see especially younger people to be quite assured that they don't need to define themselves ... it kind of opened my eyes it was like "Wow." So you realize how constructive your mind is to 40 years of a binary society that says "That's male, that's female, and that's the sick trans person, that's it there's nothing else," so ... I realized how narrow my mind was.' (Holly)

Holly looked at YouTube videos as well but found that Instagram was specifically helpful. As a 40-year-old, Instagram helped her make friends with younger trans people that she may never have met offline. These younger people introduced her to the concept of being non-binary and showed her different models of transness at a time when she was struggling to understand her gender. She knew she was trans and feminine but the label of trans woman did not feel right and the community she found on Instagram helped broaden her concept of gender and understand her own experience of gender more fully.

Ruth Pearce found that Twitter is another site where trans knowledges are shared and legitimated. She specifically looked at the use of #transdocfail, a hashtag used primarily by trans people sharing their negative healthcare experiences. She found that 'a unifying feature across the hashtag's approximately two thousand tweets is the promotion of personal trans knowledges and experiences as credible … Twitter therefore provides a platform for individual accounts to be collectively and mutually (re)constructed as credible, with these knowledges affirmed through iterative repetition in a public space' (Pearce, 2018: 172). This social media platform provides not only a valuable resource for the trans reader of the hashtag (which doctors to avoid, what experiences to expect, and so on) but also a refreshing opportunity to have their experience believed and regarded as important for the trans person sending the tweet.

Some participants also made use of Twitter in a different way. Flora follows their private gender specialist on the platform to keep up with any practice updates that may be relevant to them. At a time when they were not happy with how difficult it was to get ahold of the practice they saw a post on Twitter of the team in the pub for a 'secretary meeting' as quoted in Chapter 5. Of course it is possible that this post was a joke and Flora did find it a bit funny, but they also found it to be quite telling. To them it explained the difficulties they were having reaching the secretaries and painted the practice as somewhat unprofessional in their eyes. Trans people are not only using social media to get information from other trans people, they are also using it to get information directly from medical care providers, in this case via monitoring their publicly posted content.

In the same way Holly used Instagram to connect with fellow trans people, Ingrid has used Twitter to connect with potential care providers. When we spoke she was in the process of trying to access continuing hormone replacement therapy as her current private provider is retiring soon. She was struggling to get a prescription through her GP and reached out to another private provider but received no response. Being many years on hormones and post bottom surgery, she believes this is because that provider is "just not interested in dealing with somebody who just needs a hormone prescription, she's looking for people who want to go through the whole system" (Ingrid). She was becoming worried that her hormone regime would be interrupted so she was planning to get in touch with another private provider that she was familiar with online: "I know [him] a bit from Twitter so I'm hoping that an email to them might actually get me a prescription, failing that black market probably" (Ingrid). She was hoping that her online connection with this provider will mean she won't be ignored like she was with the other practice. If that is unsuccessful, however, she recognizes that accessing hormones without a prescription will have to be her last resort. Holly and Flora are both self-curating a mixture of professional (calling and emailing care providers directly) and social (Twitter) communication to access healthcare and information.

Getting information online is not always a positive experience. Ben recalled looking up trans experiences the first time he tried to start his transition when he was 19. He found some information, but did not learn the skills to navigate the NHS bureaucracy. He approached his GP hoping to get referred to a gender clinic but his GP refused and insisted he was not trans. Not being armed with enough information and not being as assertive in his own estimation as he is today, he accepted the GP's decision and did not pursue his transition for a few more years.

> 'I think I was aware of testosterone but I had all these strange ideas because … you're just scrambling around in the dark really. You're just looking for things online and certain people say some things and then you get confused who's who and everything. So I was taking information from like both sides, so trans women were talking and I was confused, I was like, "Is that me?", like I didn't know what the terms were, I didn't know … any of these things. Like I kind of had this idea in my head that testosterone, you take it for five years and then you're good, like you don't have to take it again, because somebody online said that, you know the maximum effects happen after five years or something. So for like two years I thought that's what the deal was, I can take it five years and then I'm good to go. But I was completely in the dark and that first experience was pretty dire for me, I guess I think if I had been more clued up, if I understood what I was actually going for, then it wouldn't have been so bad. But because I was literally just reaching out to this person … I didn't have anything in mind, I didn't think "Oh I wanna get on testosterone", I was just like "I need some help, like I'm feeling terrible." I was just literally asking for help and they totally shut me down.' (Ben)

Ben had access to all of this great information but not to a community or anyone to contextualize and explain it. He learned that for most people they stop seeing changes after a few years on testosterone, which is true. However he was missing further information, that you can lose some of those changes by stopping hormones and the risks of not maintaining hormone levels. The education here was decentralized but it was not social and both aspects are important for TransLiteracy. Without that crucial element he became more confused and did not have the tools to advocate for himself more fiercely with his GP at the time.

Offline education

Being able to learn and make use of all this information to self-advocate is a skill within itself that trans people acquire to access their healthcare. While some of the information is used online (sending emails to care providers, downloading forms, and so on) much is also used over the phone and in person. In this way trans people also learn by doing. Their experiences with healthcare providers inform future tactics for accessing healthcare and give them information which they can later pass along to other trans people. For example, if someone goes to their GP to get referred to a GIC and they get asked certain questions, they will be more prepared to answer those same questions once they get to the GIC. If their GP outright refuses to give them a referral, they can then warn other trans people to avoid that GP. This information can be distributed online but there are also important offline modes of teaching that trans people use, specifically in-person support groups, social events, activism, and informal discussions between friends. For Dan, meeting other trans men in person was an important learning experience. He explains:

> 'I'd started to meet other trans guys, cause up until that point I didn't know any other trans guys, and I listened to everyone else's experience and everyone else's recommendations and then you know I'm doing my own research and actually it's it is quite hard if you don't know exactly what you're looking for to see what you're supposed to get and or what route should be or which testosterone is gonna be better.' (Dan)

Dan continues to attend trans support groups and meet-ups to continue to learn and to share what he has learned with others. Flora had the experience of having a trans person in their life prior to realizing they were trans. They learned a lot about the process of accessing transition related healthcare from their long-term partner who is a trans man. While that knowledge was useful, having a trans partner did not help them realize they were trans.

> '[P]eople sort of say to me "Oh was it, was it [your partner] who made you realize that" and I'm like "No" because he's so binary that I, you know we have similar, I mean we're both on hormones, we've got similar identities but, no. Because we both went to the same all girls' school and it was the most traumatizing thing in the world for him as you can imagine a boy in an all girls' school, but for me it was

fine. Cause I guess I'm such a feminine person I fitted in and yeah I had problems with like puberty and with getting curves and just not understanding and hating it and just like periods and being like "What the fuck" … but because I'm gender fluid and I can still connect with the inner, I can connect in my own way to girlhood and I guess the beginnings of womanhood … whereas … that for him is like alien and just, you know, completely like dividing line.' (Flora)

Flora did not see themselves in their partner's experience and so did not realize at first that they could be trans as well. I had a similar experience in school where the first, and for a long time only, out trans person I knew was a trans boy in the grade above me. His experiences, such as being so certain he was a boy (I was merely certain I wasn't a girl) and being excited to start testosterone (I was unsure about the changes that testosterone brings) were so different from what I felt that I did not realize that I could be trans as well. Of course as I grew up and met more trans people I realized how diverse of an umbrella it is, but these experiences that Flora and I have had highlight the importance of being able to find possibility models that you can relate to.

One of the wonderful surprises that has come from this research has been how much the participants have taught me, not just about their own experiences but they have passed along information that will help me navigate being trans in this country. Within the interviews themselves, this exact model of social, decentralized pedagogy was taking place. Dan taught me about a new method for phalloplasty that I had not heard of before. Carey told me how to go about finding an affordable, queer-friendly therapist. Adam was going through the early appointments at his GIC when I interviewed him and he helped me decide to be referred to that same GIC and gave me a rundown of who all the people there were and how to navigate their different personalities. He also introduced me to the ins and outs of gel testosterone and the possibilities for taking lower doses with that method. Flora, who is taking low dose testosterone themselves, relayed their experience with it in generous detail which has helped me consider the same treatment for myself. Flora and I also stayed and talked at length after the interview, as they were an undergraduate student at the time, I was able to offer them some of my own experience dealing with the university system as a non-binary, transmasculine person. George gave me advice on options for freezing eggs and recommended the fertility clinic him and his partner used as being trans-friendly. As we were both engaged to be married at the time, after the interview I was also able to give him some advice regarding navigating wedding bureaucracies as a transmasculine person. Ingrid gave me valuable insights on challenges I may face as an older trans person and when I have progressed farther toward my transition goals. Emily has a lot of inside knowledge into the NHS and provided me with information on what specifically the GICs are looking for that may be useful when I start going through that process. Holly also had some useful first-hand information as a healthcare worker. Ben taught me how to make sure your blood work is done correctly and how to decode the results when testing testosterone levels. He also informed me that in his experience private providers are more supportive and clued me in to how that process works and how much it would cost should I want to go that route. These are only the key learning moments that have come as a result of this research project, there are countless more that have emerged from unrelated interactions within trans communities. Much of this information is relevant to me and will likely help me at some stage of navigating my healthcare as a trans person. Even the information that I will not personally need, the more I know the more I can pass on to other trans people I come across who may need that information.

Looking forward

As a product of trans communities that will be fed back into trans communities, this book is another form of exactly what I am discussing throughout this chapter. Indeed, the promotion of TransLiteracy is a key goal of this book, as I discussed in the Introduction. It is crucial to make the lessons of this book accessible to trans communities so they can make use of them, whether that be in a practical (such as learning how to best access transition related healthcare) or theoretical (such as rethinking how sex operates socially) way. This sharing of knowledges, self and peer education, and community building are an integral part of my research methodology as I discussed in Chapter 1. These methods can also promote and develop new ways of understanding sex and gender (Chapter 3), are contributing to the demedicalization of transness through education and community organization (Chapter 4), and can help individuals navigate complex medical bureaucracies, negotiate time, and navigate spaces (Chapter 5). It is through this social and decentralized pedagogy that trans people have been able to develop their TransLiteracy and thus improve their health and ease their access to healthcare. It is crucial that this form of pedagogy not only continues but becomes more accessible to more and more participants.

Conclusion

A trans healthcare system

Throughout this book, I have shown what it is like to navigate cisnormative healthcare systems as a trans person. But what would it look like to navigate a healthcare system that presumed a trans patient? Even if it is just a healthcare system that acknowledges the possibility of a trans patient there would be some major differences. As a standard across health services titles would be written in just like names and would not be changed by admin staff upon seeing the patient's gender marker.[1] Names and titles would also be easily changed. In terms of gender markers, sex and gender history would be recorded with more detail or perhaps there would be no need to record a patient's sex and/or gender at all. Relevant body parts (that is, cervix, prostate, breast tissue) would be included in forms to offer correct cancer screenings and other care and these records would be kept up to date following any surgeries. It would be common practice to ask for or consult notes to determine a patient's pronouns before consultations. In general there would be less multiple choice and more open-ended questions on forms and in appointments. There would be flexible ward assignments in hospitals. Most importantly, however, transness would not be considered a disorder and transition related healthcare services would be provided on an informed consent basis. It is this idealistic but nevertheless easily imaginable scenario that I describe in the following section.

The tension of demedicalization

In Chapter 4 I unpacked the medicalization of transness and the harm it causes through stigmatization and creating barriers to healthcare access, while in Chapter 5 I addressed some of the axes of power that are at play because transness is medicalized. I outlined the gatekeeping practices, bureaucratic processes, long and uncertain wait times for care, and gendered spaces which all put up further barriers between trans people and good health outcomes. It is on this basis that I argue for demedicalization, where transness would cease to be labeled as a disorder and transition related healthcare would no longer be provided under the banner of 'treatments'. Here is where the central tension of this argument lies. If demedicalization is the answer to the harms of medicalization, then what are trans people who rely on being able to access medical technologies to do? While I do see how demedicalization and access to transition related healthcare are at odds within current healthcare systems, I do not believe that it needs to be that way. A model of accessing medical technologies which is based on informed consent at every stage would be able to accomplish both of these goals. Rather than being assessed via multiple third parties to determine what care is allowed, there would be a self-assessment. For a trans man seeking top surgery, for example, this self-assessment would be as simple as deciding that they want and/or need their breasts removed.[2] They would then refer themselves to the surgeon of their choice in a similar fashion to the process for self-referral to physiotherapy which I outlined in Chapter 5. The surgeon would then obtain informed consent and perform the procedure. This is not as big a shift as it may seem. Other aspects of human diversity have already been demedicalized (like homosexuality) and other services already operate on self-referral (like physiotherapy). Self-assessment and informed consent are already aspects of the process for accessing transition related healthcare, thus, this model is simply about removing the other aspects of the process that serve as barriers, namely long wait times for appointments with multiple third party gatekeepers who are applying inconsistent and often inaccurate definitions of gender and embodiment. I cannot say how likely this model is to come into effect, but if the barriers to quality healthcare and good health outcomes are not identified and alternative models are not proposed then things will certainly never change.

Concluding summaries

Methodology

In Chapter 1, I laid out a model for a trans methodology which I have worked toward in this research and will continue to develop in future projects. This is one of the most broadly applicable contributions of this work as it can be applied to many fields of research, particularly those that study marginalized groups. This model has four components. Firstly, the research is completed within the communities. This includes research on trans people being done by trans people but it can also expand to research on race and racism being done by people of color, research on disability being done by disabled people, research on refugees being done by refugees, and so on. I believe that the access granted to a community member, the intimate first-hand knowledge of the topic, and the lack of a fascination with and presumed expertise of 'the other' are valuable tools that can produce rich research data. The second feature is that interviews (and other first-hand narrative accounts such as autobiographies) are particularly valuable. The key is allowing trans people, or whoever is being researched, to give their experience in their own words. Trans people are the preeminent experts on their own experience and an important part of this work is demonstrating that and valuing trans knowledges. In combination with the first component, this allows for the use of autoethnography as I have done here. Thirdly, research using this methodology would deploy a trans writing style as I have demonstrated throughout this book. Two of its key features are not presuming to be able to determine someone's gender without them articulating it themselves and keeping everything rooted in the current moment, recognizing that things have and will continue to change. The fourth component of this trans methodology is that the findings are fed back into the communities in an accessible way. This includes publicly accessible presentations, open access publications, and summaries in easy to read language which can be disseminated online or in print in community spaces. It is this outline for a trans methodology that I hope to continue to employ and build on throughout my career and thus I consider it one of the key findings of this research.

Sex and gender

Chapters 2 and 3 worked toward a better understanding of sex and gender and the way those two concepts relate to each other. This is crucial as it is this understanding on which the rest of the book operates. The conclusion I drew in those chapters is that the sex and gender distinction, while at one time practical, is no longer useful. Sex and gender are in fact intimately related in that gender can influence sex. This is possible because sex as well as gender is socially constructed and self-determined. Both have deeply important social meanings and are constructed and articulated individually through practices of gendered presentation, embodiment, and intra-action. Both sex and gender being self-determined and self-determinable paves the way for both morphological self-determination and thus the informed consent model of accessing medical technologies that I discussed here and for trans people who do not wish to alter their bodies in the linear, binary way or in any way at all. It is an important opening up of possibilities that allow for greater human diversity and challenges existing classificatory systems.

TransLiteracy

Another key finding comes from Chapter 6 where I described TransLiteracy, or the sum of the skills and knowledge trans people accumulate in order to access quality healthcare and good health outcomes, and how it is disseminated and received. Just as with the methodology, this concept could be applied more broadly to understand the specific knowledges any marginalized group accumulates to navigate healthcare systems. Seeing how this community education occurs, in a social and decentralized manner, has practical as well as theoretical implications. Valuing and promoting this type of pedagogy, which takes place outside of any one institution, has flexible and overlapping understandings of 'teacher' and 'student', and is contextualized within communities could help trans people overcome barriers to good health outcomes until those barriers can be removed.

Limitations

The most prominent limitations of this research are the various limitations of the participant group. While each voice in this research is valuable and important, it is still a relatively small group of interviewees. That group is also limited to English speakers as I regretfully only speak English and it is heavily biased toward Londoners. While not every participant lives in or is from London, me being based in London for the duration of this project has limited the participation pool. With more time and resources for recruitment, future research where more interviews could be conducted would build on this work significantly. Additionally, the participants were majority white, transmasculine, and under 35. I cannot say for certain why this is the case, but it is not lost on me that I am also white, transmasculine, and under 35. Future additions to this work and trans studies in general would benefit from the voices of more Black people, people of color, trans women, transfeminine people, young people, older people, and people at various intersections thereof. In order to accomplish this more targeted recruitment will need to take place and potential issues of accessibility and safety will need to be addressed. The specifics of these measures could be worked out in communities, but they may include providing compensation for the time it takes to participate, interviewing people in their own homes or in other more private locations, and reaching out to various minority support groups rather than just general trans groups. Finally, I was also limited in fully understanding the diversity of my participant pool by only tracking age, race, gender, and pronouns. In future research I will collect more information about socioeconomic class, religious affiliation/belief, immigration history, disability and health, educational attainment, work, and so on, in order to ensure a diversity of perspectives and to see where in-group patterns may emerge.

Final thoughts

At the heart of this book is a call to action. Trans people in the UK are not being served by healthcare systems in ways that are respectful, timely, or attentive to their specific needs. One participant, Holly, perfectly summarized the ethos of this entire project when she said "this individual have the right to be protected. A transgender individual … or non-binary, wherever they come from, have the right to be treated equally with respect and a knowledge in the way they want". It is this idea, that trans people deserve equal access to quality healthcare, delivered in a respectful manner by knowledgeable providers, which led me to this work in the first place. Throughout this project I have come not only to the conclusions discussed in this chapter but also to a new understanding of my role as a scholar in my communities. Seeking ways to use scholarship to address problems like these, rather than simply to document them, is the best use I can imagine for my career and is something which I hope will become a lifelong project.

Notes

Introduction

1. I am following Ruth Pearce (2018) here in using the plural 'communities' to avoid misrepresenting trans people as a monolith.
2. *The Birth of the Clinic: An Archaeology of Medical Perception* was first published in French in 1963 (as *Naissance de la clinique: une archéologie du regard médical*) but the English translation was published in 1973.
3. I am referring here to the ability for people to easily share information with very few barriers to publication. This is in contrast to, for example, information that is published in an academic journal or a newspaper. There is of course gatekeeping that happens on these sites with algorithms determining what shows up in feeds and search results, however that is distinct from the gatekeeping of what gets published in the first place that happens with other sources of knowledge. Additionally, many of the examples I will discuss in Chapter 6 concern content that is found through very specific searches or is published within smaller online communities, such as secret Facebook groups, which bypasses some of these issues.
4. The work that this quote is from is in fact about a trans woman, however at the time of writing it Garfinkel and the rest of the researchers working on this case believed the subject to be an intersex person so that is the perspective they were writing from.
5. Although this does not eliminate class-based health inequalities (see Gray, 1982).
6. Within the NHS, '[c]ommissioning is the continual process of planning, agreeing and monitoring services' (NHS, 2019). It is how the NHS decides what services are needed and who will provide those services and in what ways.

Chapter 1

1. I define 'trans' as I am using it here and address some of the limitations of this term in Chapter 2, but in short, 'trans' is simply the umbrella term I have chosen. Another scholar may identify themselves and/or their participants with a different umbrella term (such as J.R. Latham who uses the term 'transexual') but could still fall under this methodology if discussing the same communities.
2. 'Privilege' here refers to social advantages experienced by groups of people based on their having certain characteristic(s). Palczewski et al define privileges as 'unearned freedoms or opportunities. Often, privileges are unconscious and unmarked. They are made to appear natural and normal through cultural hegemony, which makes them easy to deny and more resistant to change' (2017: 31). See also McIntosh (1988, 2015).
3. This is a play on feminist film scholar Laura Mulvey's concept of the 'male gaze' in which they argue that women are always-already viewed and presented (in Mulvey's focus in film) from the perspective of and for the enjoyment of heterosexual men as the dominant social group (1975). I am translating this famous term here to apply to cis people as the dominant social group (à la Cava, 2016) and expanding it beyond film to include representation of the marginalized social group (in this case trans people) in other mediums, specifically research outputs.
4. *Testo Junkie* was originally published in Spanish in 2008 but I am referencing the 2013 English publication.
5. While Feminist Standpoint Theory has not been a specific inspiration here, the methodology that I propose does share similarities with it. Both methodologies work to

recast marginalized groups as active subjects who take part in knowledge production, rather than as merely objects available to the research scrutiny of outside 'experts' (Harding, 2004).

[6] While this is not one of the main features of this methodology, it is interdisciplinary both in the sense that it can be applied throughout different disciplines as well as that it is advantageous to draw knowledge from different disciplines as I discussed in the Introduction.

[7] Harris is referring here to the spread of CRT in the United States. However, it has also gained international popularity, including in the UK where this research is based (Chakrabarty et al, 2012).

[8] See Grillo and Wildman's 1991 article, 'Obscuring the Importance of Race: The Implication of Making Comparisons Between Racism and Sexism (Or Other-Isms)', for more on the pitfalls of specifically comparing all forms of oppression to racism.

[9] Chang also warns of the following pitfalls of autoethnography, '(1) excessive focus on the self in isolation from others; (2) overemphasis on narration rather than analysis and cultural interpretation; (3) exclusive reliance on personal memory and recalling as a data source; (4) negligence of ethical standards regarding others in self-narratives; and (5) inappropriate application of the label "autoethnography"' (2016: 54). I have tried to be cognizant of all of these throughout this research, particularly in relation to consulting with other community members to combat isolation of the self, writing about experiences as they were happening whenever possible, and tying every narration into a larger framework of interpretation.

[10] I am using Nancy Naples' understanding of insider research, which defines it simply as 'the study of one's own social group or society' (2003: 46).

Chapter 2

[1] An example of early work understanding transness through the lens of a sex/gender distinction can be found in Robert J. Stoller's 1968 book *Sex and Gender: The Development of Masculinity and Femininity* and an important foundational unpacking and questioning of that distinction can be found in West and Zimmerman's 1987 article, 'Doing Gender'.

[2] This concept directly relates to medicalization, where a trans person's sex and gender are seen as being at odds with each other (gender dysphoria) and the treatment is to bring them back into alignment through medical intervention, a model that requires the separation of the concepts of sex and gender. This will be discussed at length in Chapter 4.

[3] It is important to note that all of the concepts discussed in this chapter do not only apply to trans people. Everyone has a body and a relationship to gender but trans experiences highlight these concepts in a unique and productive way.

[4] Some trans people may always retain the gamete production system they were born with, meaning they may, for example, both possess egg cells and not produce sperm cells, thereby carrying both gendered signifiers of, in this case, a 'female' gamete production system.

[5] This does not mean that non-binary people never endeavor to change their bodies and never experience a 'wrong body' narrative, indeed many do. The disruption comes instead from the fact that if they do want/need to change their bodies, there is not a culturally legible ideal non-binary body for them to move toward. The 'wrong body' narrative, as Bettcher explains, depicts trans women moving toward an ideal female body and trans men moving toward an ideal male body. Of course, many trans women and trans men will also individually challenge this narrative by choosing to forgo hormones, certain surgeries, and so on.

[6] Further important work challenging the idea that having a body that differs from expected norms means one must desire to 'fix' or change their body through medical intervention can be found in intersex (Chase, 1998; Karkazis, 2008), disability (McRuer,

2006; Overboe, 2009; Davis, 2016), and fat (Murray, 2008; Lupton, 2013; Burford and Orchard, 2014) scholarship.

Chapter 3

1. Perhaps barring identical twins but that's beside the point.
2. These characteristics were 'long hair, short hair, wide hips, narrow hips, breasts, flat chest, body hair, penis, vulva, "unisex" shirt, and "unisex" pants' (Kessler and McKenna, 1978/2006: 168).
3. Cisnormativity is the assumption that everyone is cisgender. For example, a doctor automatically referring a woman for cervical screening and not referring a man is cisnormative because assuming that all women and only women have cervixes ignores the transfeminine people who do not need such services and the transmasculine people who do. It is used to typify the healthcare system here because as a transmasculine person Ben was an unexpected variance that the care providers could not make sense of.
4. Before beginning testosterone, trans people undergoing this type of hormone therapy are given a blood test to check existing testosterone levels, liver functioning, and other relevant markers.
5. Metoidioplasty is a surgical procedure where what is referred to as the clitoris (which will become larger from taking testosterone) is made into what is referred to as a penis by detaching it from the labia minora. It is a simpler alternative to phalloplasty that does not require a skin graft, so it therefore results in a smaller penis. It is often accompanied by a scrotoplasty where the labia majora are formed into what is referred to as a scrotum with the use of silicon implants.
6. Trans people sometimes use different words to refer to their body parts, particularly those that carry heavily gendered connotations such as 'clitoris' or 'penis'.
7. I go into how ticking boxes operates as a feature of the medical bureaucracy in Chapter 5.
8. In this article, Case uses the term gender to refer more to gender expression and degrees of masculinity and femininity than an individual's stated gender identity.
9. Title IX is the federal statute in the United States banning sex discrimination in federally funded programs (U.S. Department of Education Office for Civil Rights, 2015).
10. A packer is a prosthetic penis primarily used to create a bulge.
11. A strap-on refers to a prosthetic penis specifically used for sexual play.
12. Tucking refers to any method of concealing a penis and testicles.
13. Binding is the practice of wearing a compression garment to flatten the chest.
14. Partial only in the eyes of the medicalized model of transness. A trans man who, for example, goes on testosterone and never has any surgery would, if that's all they require, have undergone a complete transition.
15. According to the National Transgender Discrimination Survey, conducted in 2010 in the United States, 41 percent of participants had attempted suicide compared to 1.6 percent of the general population. The Trans Mental Health Study, a smaller scale study conducted in the UK in 2012, found that 35 percent of participants had attempted suicide at least once and 25 percent more than once. They also found that suicidal ideation and attempts decreased after transition (McNeil et al, 2012).
16. Which he explains were not related to his transness at all but stemmed from past trauma and childhood abuse.

Chapter 4

1. I delve into the specifics of these bureaucratic barriers in the following chapter.
2. In this case, part of the medicalizing process is the naming of the illness. Some may argue that transness per se is not being medicalized here, and that, rather, it is the illness of

gender identity disorder (or gender dysphoria or any other name it may go by). However, I argue that there is no gender identity disorder without transness. Thus, what is being medicalized is having gender identity different from the one usually associated with the sex one was assigned at birth. In this way it is transness that is medicalized.

3 As mentioned previously, trans people were at risk of falling afoul of anti-gay laws. For a history of this legislation in the UK see Peter Tatchell's 2017 *Guardian* article, 'Don't Fall for the Myth that it's 50 Years Since We Decriminalised Homosexuality'.

4 Additionally, this raises questions about what types of relationships the state sees as viable, specifically a disregard for the possibility that someone would want to stay married upon finding out that their spouse's gender is different from what they thought it was when they got married.

5 This term is no longer officially in use by the NHS but it is still used by many clinicians to refer to social transition and many participants recounted this term being used to frame their GIC care.

6 Some GICs do now accept self-referral, which is a welcome change, but not all of them do and since this is a recent change people might not be aware that they are able to self-refer. All of the participants in this research accessed GICs when self-referral was not an option.

7 While top surgery (breast augmentation) is a necessary step for many transfeminine people it is not routinely provided by the NHS.

8 I go into more detail about these bureaucratic processes in Chapter 5.

9 This book was originally published in French in 1966 under the title *Le Normal et le Pathologique* but I am referencing Carolyn R. Fawcett's 1991 translation here.

10 Access to therapy and mental health services would be easier as those are separately existing parts of the NHS.

11 For example this happened at Harry Benjamin's clinic in the 1960s which I discuss in more detail in Chapter 6 (Stone, 1991/2006).

12 A British celebrity with famously large, surgically enhanced breasts.

13 See Cundill and Wiggins (2017) for an example of the informed consent model as it applies to hormone replacement therapy, however I would expand this to include puberty blockers and surgeries as well.

14 This depathologization is supported by many clinicians working in the GICs, as I discussed in the Introduction.

15 Interventions being redefined as non-medical removes them from the framework of being treatments for an illness that requires a diagnosis. This does not mean that they are removed from the framework of expertise. Surgical interventions in particular would still need to be carried out by highly qualified, trained, and ethical experts. As Ben Vincent notes, '[e]ven under [an informed consent] system, guidance, support, and competent practice are still absolutely needed' (2018: 190).

16 As I explained earlier, the informed consent model can be used to access interventions from skilled practitioners beyond the framework of illness and treatment.

Chapter 5

1 I use the more colloquial phrase 'jumping through hoops' because this specific phrasing was used by one of my participants and it concisely encapsulates the idea of having to complete a series of actions which are either purposeless or where the person completing them is unaware of the purpose.

2 There is now a gender service operating in Wales.

3 As I discussed in the introduction, the GICs have mental health professionals as part of their multidisciplinary teams, however they are not commissioned to offer therapy or any psychological support that is not related to gender and/or transition.

Notes

4   See Vincent (2018) for an in-depth look at the referral process for all GICs as of late 2017.
5   J.R. Latham also addresses this dichotomy between breast reduction and double mastectomy in their 2017 article 'Making and Treating Trans Problems: The Ontological Politics of Clinical Practices'.
6   Although trans people also access breast reductions for various reasons.
7   This strategy of selectively deploying personal narrative will be discussed in more detail in Chapter 6.
8   Eschaton is the end of the world.
9   I discuss these support networks in more detail in Chapter 6.

Chapter 6

1   This is just one possible way of overcoming barriers. Of course there are other ways and some people face barriers which they never overcome. Additionally, it is possible that accessing information in this way could create barriers, which I discuss below, referencing Ruth Pearce's work on negative discourses.
2   Namely the UK, mostly London, between 2016 and 2018.
3   The portion of the internet where users interact with each other (a part of Web 2.0). In this chapter I will be primarily referring to YouTube, Facebook, Twitter, and Instagram, although this is not to say there is not important community building and education happening on other platforms.
4   While Latham and I are specifically discussing trans penises here, the equation can apply to cis men as well, many of whom have the added benefit of others confirming their narrative understanding of their normative penis throughout their lives.
5   Although there are certainly trans people who have what is usually referred to as a penis for whom that penis is part of their identity construction and therefore they fall into the phallus + narrative category.
6   Cowell maintained that she was intersex in her autobiography (Cowell, 1954) so she may have been intersex and trans. However, as presenting as intersex was the only way she could have accessed transition related healthcare it is also possible that she was deploying a similar strategy to Agnes.
7   While I do define some basic trans terminology throughout this book, a full linguistic analysis would be beyond the scope of this work. A body of work as extensive as Paul Baker's (2002) writing on Polari (British slang used by gay people in the mid 20th century) could be written about contemporary trans communication.
8   Much more could and has been written on the various forms of online harassment faced by trans people, however within the scope of this chapter I am focusing on how trans people and communities use the internet as a tool to overcome healthcare barriers.
9   Kat Blaque is a Black trans woman who uses her YouTube channel to speak about many feminist and political issues.
10 Deadnaming is calling a trans person by the name they were given at birth (or any old name) after they have changed their name to one that is more comfortably gendered for them. When this is done maliciously it is a way of invalidating the person's gender by refusing to call them their chosen name.
11 Michael Rich and Richard Chalfen similarly found that the combination of the auditory and the visual was advantageous in their 1999 study on children with asthma educating healthcare providers through the creation of videos.
12 Internet usage may be restricted by only being able to access the internet on public computers, having internet usage surveilled by family members, and so on.
13 There are unlisted and private videos, but from the perspective of the typical user YouTube is an open, public platform.

14. When creating a Facebook group you have one of three options for the level of privacy. The first is to make it 'public', meaning anyone see the group, who is in it, and the posts. The second level of privacy would be a 'closed' group where anyone can search for and find the group and see who is in it but only members can read the posts. The final option is a 'secret' group where only members can find the group, see who is in it, and read the posts. In order to join a closed group you would only need to search for the group, request to join, and have an admin accept the request. However, to join a secret group you need to be invited to join by a current member of the group and approved by an admin.
15. These types of closed and secret Facebook groups which are limited to people with a certain shared experience are important sites of information sharing, support, and organization. There are Facebook groups for young people with attention deficit hyperactivity disorder (Gajaria et al, 2011), parents of premature babies (Thoren et al, 2013), people with breast cancer (Bender et al, 2011) and many more such shared experiences.
16. 'Gender euphoria' is used by some trans people to describe the feeling of being super comfortable in your expression/body and/or having your gender affirmed. For example one might say that a stranger correctly gendering them or pulling off the perfect smoky eye gave them gender euphoria. It is a play on (and in some cases a resistance against) the term 'gender dysphoria'.
17. See Pi et al (2013) for more on what motivates people to share knowledge in Facebook groups.

Conclusion

1. At every GP I have registered with since starting to use Mx. as my title, that has not been an option so I use Mr. as it is my second choice. However, every time my title ends up being changed to Miss or Ms. without my consent. When I question this I have been told that it is because of the 'F' marker in my records.
2. This step already occurs when an individual is deciding to be referred to a GIC or is deciding which referrals they are going to request from the GIC.

References

Abraham, J. (2009) 'The Pharmaceutical Industry, the State and the NHS', in Gabe, J. and Calnan, M. (eds) *The New Sociology of the Health Service*, Oxon: Routledge, pp 99–120.

Achermann, E. and Achermann, J. (2014) 'When Your Baby is Born with Genitals that Look Different … The First Days', *DSD Families*. Available at: https://dsdfamilies.org/application/files/1615/4236/8548/firstdays-dsdfamilies.pdf#:~:text=A%20good%20way%20to%20think,variations%20in%20the%20baby's%20chromosomes (Accessed September 7, 2023).

Adam, B. (2004) *Time*, Cambridge: Polity Press.

Adams, M.A. (2015) 'Traversing the Transcape: A Brief Historical Etymology of Trans Terminology', in Capuzza, J.C. and Spencer, L.G. (eds) *Transgender Communication Studies: Histories, Trends, and Trajectories*, London: Lexington Books, pp 173–185.

Adams, T.E., Jones, S.H., and Ellis, C. (2014) *Autoethnography: Understanding Qualitative Research*, Oxford: Oxford University Press.

Ahmed, S.F., Achermann, J.C., Arlt, W., Balen, A.H., Conway, G., Edwards, Z.L., Elford, S., Hughes, I.A., Izatt, L., Krone, N., Miles, H.L., O'Toole, S., Perry, L., Sanders, C., Simmonds, M., Wallace, A.M., Watt, A., and Willis, D. (2011) 'UK Guidance on the Initial Evaluation of an Infant or an Adolescent with a Suspected Disorder of Sex Development', *Clinical Endocrinology*, 75(1): 12–26.

Andrews, J. (2014) *Showing Off! A Philosophy of Image*, London: Bloomsbury.

Annamma, S.A., Connor, D., and Ferri, B. (2012) 'Dis/ability Critical Race Studies (DisCrit): Theorizing at the Intersections of Race and Dis/ability', *Race Ethnicity and Education*, 16(1): 1–31.

Arksey, H. (1994) 'Expert and Lay Participation in the Construction of Medical Knowledge', *Sociology of Health and Illness*, 16(4): 448–468.

Badgett, M.V.L., Lau, H., Sears, B., and Ho, D. (2007) *Bias in the Workplace: Consistent Evidence of Sexual Orientation and Gender Identity Discrimination*, Los Angeles: The Williams Institute UCLA School of Law.

Baker, P. (2002) *Polari: The Lost Language of Gay Men*, London: Routledge.

Ballard, K. and Elston, M.A. (2005) 'Medicalisation: A Multi-dimensional Concept', *Social Theory & Health*, 3(3): 228–241.

Barad, K. (2003) 'Posthumanist Performativity: Toward an Understanding of How Matter Comes to Matter', *Signs: Journal of Women in Culture and Society*, 28(3): 801–831.

Barcelos, C.A. and Budge, S.L. (2019) 'Inequalities in Crowdfunding for Transgender Health Care', *Transgender Health*, 4(1): 81–88.

Barker, K.K. (1998) 'A Ship Upon a Stormy Sea: The Medicalization of Pregnancy', *Social Science & Medicine*, 47(8): 1067–1076.

Beasley, C. and Flory, D. (2009) *From the Chief Nursing Officer and Director General NHS Finance, Performance and Operations*, Department of Health. Available at: https://assets.publishing.service.gov.uk/government/uploads/system/uploads/ attachment_data/file/200215/CNO_note_dh_098893.pdf (Accessed September 7, 2023).

Bender, J.L., Jimenez-Marroquin, M., and Jadad, A.R. (2011) 'Seeking Support on Facebook: A Content Analysis of Breast Cancer Groups', *Journal of Medical Internet Research*, 13(1): e16.

Bettcher, T.M. (2014) 'Trapped in the Wrong Theory: Rethinking Trans Oppression and Resistance', *Signs*, 39(2): 383–406.

Blackless, M., Charuvastra, A., Derryck, A., Fausto-Sterling, A., Lauzanne, K., and Lee, E. (2000) 'How Sexually Dimorphic Are We? Review and Synthesis', *American Journal of Human Biology*, 12(2): 151–166.

Bornstein, K. (1994) *Gender Outlaw*, New York: Routledge.

Bouman, W.P. and Richards, C. (2013) 'Diagnostic and Treatment Issues for People with Gender Dysphoria in the United Kingdom', *Sexual and Relationship Therapy*, 28(3): 165–171.

Bouman, W.P., Richards, C., Addinall, R.M., Arango de Montis, I., Arcelus, J., Duisin, D., Esteva, I., Fisher, A., Harte, F., Khoury, B., Lu, Z., Marais, A., Mattila, A., Nayarana Reddy, D., Nieder, T.O., Robles Garcia, R., Rodrigues Jr., O.M., Roque Guerra, A., Tereshkevich, D., T'Sjoen, G., and Wilson, D. (2014) 'Yes and Yes Again: Are Standards of Care which Require Two Referrals for Genital Reconstructive Surgery Ethical?', *Sexual and Relationship Therapy*, 29(4): 377–389.

Boylorn, R.M. and Orbe, M.P. (2016) *Critical Autoethnography: Intersecting Cultural Identities in Everyday Life*, Oxon: Routledge.

Bradford, J., Reisner, S.L., Honnold, J.A., and Xavier, J. (2013) 'Experiences of Transgender-Related Discrimination and Implications for Health: Results From the Virginia Transgender Health Initiative Study', *American Journal of Public Health*, 103(10): 1820–1829.

Broom, D.H. and Woodward, R.V. (1996) 'Medicalisation Reconsidered: Toward a Collaborative Approach to Care', *Sociology of Health and Illness*, 18(3): 357–378.

Brown, J., Sorrell, J.H., McClaren, J., and Creswell, J.W. (2006) 'Waiting for a Liver Transplant', *Qualitative Health Research*, 16(1): 119–136.

Burford, J. and Orchard, S. (2014) 'Chubby Boys with Strap-Ons: Queering Fat Transmasculine Embodiment', in Pausé, C., Wykes, J., and Murray, S. (eds) *Queering Fat Embodiment*, Farnham: Ashgate, pp 61–73.

Butler, J. (1990) *Gender Trouble: Feminism and the Subversion of Identity*, New York: Routledge.

Butler, J. (2001/2006) 'Doing Justice to Someone: Sex Reassignment and Allegories of Transsexuality', in Stryker, S. and Whittle, S. (eds) *The Transgender Studies Reader*, New York: Routledge, pp 183–193.

Cacioppo, J.T. and Hawkley, L. (2003) 'Social Isolation and Health, with an Emphasis on Underlying Mechanisms', *Perspectives in Biology and Medicine*, 46(3): 39–52.

Cacioppo, J.T. and Hawkley, L. (2009) 'Perceived Social Isolation and Cognition', *Trends in Cognitive Sciences*, 13(10): 447–454.

Canguilhem, G. (1991) *The Normal and the Pathological*, Brooklyn: Zone Books.

Case, M.A.C. (1995) 'Disaggregating Gender from Sex and Sexual Orientation: The Effeminate Man in the Law and Feminist Jurisprudence', *Yale Law Journal*, 105(1): 1–105.

Cava, P. (2016) 'Cisgender and Cissexual', in Naples, N. et al (eds) *The Wiley Blackwell Encyclopedia of Gender and Sexuality Studies*, Malden, MA: Blackwell.

Chakrabarty, N., Roberts, L., and Preston, J. (2012) 'Critical Race Theory in England', *Race Ethnicity and Education*, 15(1): 1–3.

Chang, H. (2016) *Autoethnography as Method*, Oxon: Routledge.

Charlton, J.I. (2000) *Nothing About Us Without Us: Disability Oppression and Empowerment*, Berkeley: University of California Press.

Chase, C. (1998) 'Affronting Reason', in Atkins, D. (ed) *Looking Queer: Body Image and Identity in Lesbian, Bisexual, Gay, and Transgender Communities*, Binghampton: The Haworth Press, pp 205–219.

Chrisler, J.C. and Caplan, P. (2002) 'The Strange Case of Dr. Jekyll and Ms. Hyde: How PMS Became a Cultural Phenomenon and a Psychiatric Disorder', *Annual Review of Sex Research*, 13(1): 274–306.

Chrisler, J.C. and Gorman, J.A. (2015) 'The Medicalization of Women's Moods: Premenstural Syndrome and Premenstrual Dysphoric Disorder', in McHugh, M.C. and Chrisler, J.C. (eds) *The Wrong Prescription for Women: How Medicine and Media Create a 'Need' for Treatments, Drugs, and Surgery*, Santa Barbara: Praeger, pp 77–98.

Clements-Nolle, K., Marx, R., and Katz, M. (2006) 'Attempted Suicide Among Transgender Persons: The Influence of Gender-Based Discrimination and Victimization', *Journal of Homosexuality*, 51(3): 53–69.

Conrad, P. (1992) 'Medicalization and Social Control', *Annual Review of Sociology*, 18: 209–232.

Conrad, P. (2005) 'The Shifting Engines of Medicalization', *Journal of Health and Social Behavior*, 46: 3–14.

Conrad, P. (2007) *The Medicalization of Society: On the Transformation of Human Conditions into Treatable Disorders*, Baltimore: Johns Hopkins University Press.

Conrad, P. and Angell, A. (2004) 'Homosexuality and Remedicalization', *Society*, 41(5): 32–39.

Cornwell, E.Y. and Waite, L.J. (2009) 'Social Disconnectedness, Perceived Isolation, and Health among Older Adults', *Journal of Health and Social Behavior*, 50(1): 31–48.

Cowell, R.E. (1954) *Roberta Cowell's Story*, London: William Heinemann.

Crawford, L. (2015) *Transgender Architectonics: The Shape of Change in Modernist Space*, Farnham: Ashgate.

Creighton, S. (2001) 'Surgery for Intersex', *Journal of the Royal Society of Medicine*, 94: 218–220.

Cundill, P. and Wiggins, J. (2017) *Protocols for the Initiation of Hormone Therapy for Trans and Gender Diverse Patients*, Abbotsford, VIC: Equinox Gender Diverse Health Centre.

Cutler, D.M. and Lleras-Muney, A. (2006) *Education and Health: Evaluating Theories and Evidence*, Cambridge, MA: National Bureau of Economic Research.

Davis, L.J. (ed) (2016) *The Disability Studies Reader*, fifth edn, New York: Routledge.

Delgado, R. (1984) 'The Imperial Scholar: Reflections on a Review of Civil Rights Literature', *University of Pennsylvania Law Review*, 132: 561–1547.

Delgado, R. and Stefancic, J. (2017) *Critical Race Theory: An Introduction*, New York: New York University Press.

Delph-Janiurek, T. (2001) 'Sex, Talk and Making Bodies in the Science Lab', in Backett- Milburn, K. and McKie, L. (eds) *Constructing Gendered Bodies*, Basingstoke: Palgrave, pp 39–55.

Department of Health (2012) *Choice of GP Practice: The Patient Choice Scheme*. NHS England.

Department of Health (2013) *The Mandate: A Mandate from the Government to the NHS Commissioning Board: April 2013 to March 2015*. Available at: https://assets.publishing.service.gov.uk/media/5a7c556b40f0b62dffde1 6a8/13-15_mandate.pdf (Accessed September 7, 2023).

Drescher, J. (2015) 'Out of DSM: Depathologizing Homosexuality', *Behavioral Sciences*, 5(4): 565–575.

Duguay, S. (2016) '"He Has a Way Gayer Facebook Than I Do": Investigating Sexual Identity Disclosure and Context Collapse on a Social Networking Site', *New Media & Society*, 18(6): 891–907.

Dvorsky, G. and Hughes, J. (2008) *Postgenderism: Beyond the Gender Binary*, Hartford: Institute for Ethics and Emerging Technologies.

Ellis, C. (2004) *The Ethnographic I: A Methodological Novel about Autoethnography*, Walnut Creek, CA: AltaMira Press.

Erlick, E. (2019) 'On Rural Transgender Visibility', in Smith, W.W. and Thomas-Evans, M. (eds) *Representing Rural Women*, London: Lexington Books, pp 177–192.

Factor, R.J. and Rothblum, E.D. (2007) 'A Study of Transgender Adults and Their Non-Transgender Siblings on Demographic Characteristics, Social Support, and Experiences of Violence', *Journal of LGBT Health Research*, 3(3): 11–30.

Fairbairn, C., Pyper, D., Gheera, M., and Loft, P. (2020) 'Gender Recognition and the Rights of Transgender People'. Available at: https://commonslibrary.parliament.uk/research-briefings/cbp-8969/ (Accessed September 7, 2023).

Fausto-Sterling, A. (2000) *Sexing the Body: Gender Politics and the Construction of Sexuality*, New York: Basic Books.

Foucault, M. (1973) *The Birth of the Clinic: An Archaeology of Medical Perception*, Oxon: Routledge.

Gajaria, A., Yeung, E., Goodale, T., and Charach, A. (2011) 'Beliefs About Attention-Deficit/Hyperactivity Disorder and Response to Stereotypes: Youth Postings in Facebook Groups', *Journal of Adolescent Health*, 49(1): 15–20.

Garfinkel, H. (1967/2006) 'Passing and the Managed Achievement of Sex Status in an "Intersexed" Person', in Stryker, S. and Whittle, S. (eds) *The Transgender Studies Reader*, New York: Routledge, pp 58–93.

Garland, J. and Slokenberga, S. (2019) 'Protecting the Rights of Children with Intersex Conditions from Nonconsensual Gender-Conforming Medical Interventions: The View from Europe', *Medical Law Review*, 27(3): 482–508.

Gergen, M.M. and Gergen, K.J. (2002) 'Ethnographic Representation as Relationship', in Bochner, A.P. and Ellis, C. (eds) *Ethnographically Speaking: Autoethnography, Literature, and Aesthetics*, Walnut Creek: AltaMira Press.

Government Digital Service (2014) *Apply for a gender recognition certificate*. https://www.gov.uk/apply-gender-recognition-certificate.

Grant, J.M., Mottet, L.A., Tanis, J., Herman, J.L., Harrison, J., and Keisling, M. (2010) *National Transgender Discrimination Survey Report on Health and Health Care*, National Center for Transgender Equality and the National Gay and Lesbian Task Force.

Gray, A.M. (1982) 'Inequalities in Health. The Black Report: A Summary and Comment', *International Journal of Health Services*, 12(3): 349–380.

Greenberg, K. (2012) 'Still Hidden in the Closet: Trans Women and Domestic Violence', *Berkeley Journal of Gender, Law & Justice*, 27(2): 199–251.

Grillo, T. and Wildman, S.M. (1991) 'Obscuring the Importance of Race: The Implication of Making Comparisons Between Racism and Sexism (Or Other-Isms)', *Duke Law Journal*, 40(2): 397–412.

Grosz, E. (1994) *Volatile Bodies: Toward a Corporeal Feminism*, Crows Nest: Allen & Unwin.

Hall-Lande, J.A., Eisenberg, M.E., Christenson, S.L., and Neumark-Sztainer, D. (2007) 'Social Isolation, Psychological Health, and Protective Factors in Adolescence', *Adolescence*, 42(166): 265–286.

Halpern, S.A. (1990) 'Medicalization as Professional Process: Postwar Trends in Pediatrics', *Journal of Health and Social Behavior*, 31(1): 28–42.

Harding, S.G. (ed) (2001). *The Feminist Standpoin Theory Reader: Intellectual and Political Controversies*, New York: Routledge.

Harris, A. (2017) 'Foreword', in Delgado, R. and Stefancic, J. (eds) *Critical Race Theory: An Introduction*, New York: New York University Press, pp xiii–xvii.

Harrison, S. and Ahmad, W.I.U. (2000) 'Medical Autonomy and the UK State 1975 to 2025', *Sociology*, 34(1): 129–146.

Hildebrand-Chupp, R. (2020) 'More than 'canaries in the gender coal mine': A transfeminist approach to research on detransition', *The Sociological Review*, 68(4): 800–816.

Hirschfeld, M. (1910/2006) 'Selections from *The Transvestites: The Erotic Drive to Cross-Dress*', in Stryker, S. and Whittle, S. (eds) *The Transgender Studies Reader*, New York: Routledge, pp 28–39.

House of Commons Women and Equalities Committee (2016) *Transgender Equality: First Report of Session 2015–16*. Available at: https://publications.parliament.uk/pa/cm201516/cmselect/cmwomeq/390/390.pdf (Accessed September 8, 2023).

Hughes, I.A., Houk, C., Ahmed, S.F., and Lee, P.A. (2006) 'Consensus Statement on Management of Intersex Disorders', *Archives of Disease in Childhood*, 91(7): 554–563.

Hughes, J. (2006) 'Beyond the Medical Model of Gender Dysphoria to Morphological Self-determination', *Medical Ethics*, 13(1): 10–11.

Huss-Ashmore, R. (2000) '"The Real Me": Therapeutic Narrative in Cosmetic Surgery', *The Expedition*, 3(42): 27–37.

Israeli-Nevo, A. (2017) 'Taking (My) Time: Temporality in Transition, Queer Delays and Being (in the) Present', *Somatechnics*, 7(1): 34–49.

Jackson, S. and Scott, S. (2001) 'Putting the Body's Feet on the Ground: Towards a Sociological Reconceptualization of Gendered and Sexual Embodiment', in Backett-Milburn, K. and McKie, L. (eds) *Constructing Gendered Bodies*, Basingstoke: Palgrave, pp 9–24.

Jones, S.H. (2007) 'Autoethnography', in G. Ritzer (ed.) *The Blackwell Encyclopedia of Sociology*, Malden, MA: Blackwell, pp.230–232.

Jin, R.L., Chandrakant, P.S., and Tomislav, J.S. (1995) 'The Impact of Unemployment on Health: A Review of the Evidence', *Canadian Medical Association Journal*, 153(5): 529–540.

Johnson, J.L. and Repta, R. (2012) 'Sex and Gender: Beyond the Binaries', in Oliffe, J.L. and Greaves, L. (eds) *Designing and Conducting Gender, Sex, and Health Research*, Thousand Oaks, CA: SAGE, pp 17–37.

Karkazis, K. (2008) *Fixing Sex: Intersex, Medical Authority, and Lived Experience*, Durham: Duke University Press.

Kessler, S.J. and McKenna, W. (1978/2006) 'Toward a Theory of Gender', in Stryker, S. and Whittle, S. (eds) *The Transgender Studies Reader*, New York: Routledge, pp 165–182.

Kreiss, J.L. and Patterson, D.L. (1997) 'Psychosocial Issues in Primary Care of Lesbian, Gay, Bisexual, and Transgender Youth', *Journal of Pediatric Health Care*, 11(6): 266–274.

Latham, J.R. (2016) *Trans Men's Realities: An Ontological Politics of Sex, Gender and Sexuality*, PhD Thesis, Melbourne: La Trobe University.

Latham, J.R. (2017). 'Making and Treating Trans Problems: The Ontological Politics of Clinical Practices', *Studies in Gender and Sexuality*, 18(1): 40–61. doi.org/10.1080/15240657.2016.1238682

Latham, J.R. (2017) '(Re)making Sex: A Praxiography of the Gender Clinic', *Feminist Theory*, 18(2): 177–204.

Lee, C. and Kwan, P.K.Y. (2014) 'The Trans Panic Defense: Heteronormativity, and the Murder of Transgender Women', Washington, DC: George Washington University Law Faculty, pp 75–132. doi: 10.2139/ssrn.2430390.

Liao, L., Wood, D., and Creighton, S.M. (2015) 'Parental Choice on Normalising Cosmetic Genital Surgery', *BMJ: British Medical Journal*, 351. doi: 10.1136/bmj.h5124.

Lombardi, E.L., Wilchins, R.A., Priesing, D., and Malouf, D. (2002) 'Gender Violence: Transgender Experiences with Violence and Discrimination', *Journal of Homosexuality*, 42(1): 89–101.

Lorimer, S. (2018) 'Foreword', in Vincent, B., *Transgender Health: A Practitioner's Guide to Binary and Non-Binary Trans Patient Care*, London: Jessica Kingsley Publishers: 11–13.

Lupton, D. (2013) *Fat*, Oxon: Routledge.

MacDonald, M. (1989) 'The Medicalization of Suicide in England: Laymen, Physicians, and Cultural Change, 1500–1870', *The Milbank Quarterly*, 67(1): 69–91.

Maister, D.H. (2005) 'The Psychology of Waiting Lines'. Available at: https://davidmaister.com/articles/the-psychology-of-waiting-lines/ (Accessed September 7, 2023).

Martin, E. (1991) 'The Egg and the Sperm: How Science Has Constructed a Romance Based on Stereotypical Male-Female Roles', *Signs*, 16(3): 485–501.

Mattingly, C. (1994) 'The Concept of Therapeutic "Emplotment"', *Social Science & Medicine*, 38(6): 811–822.

McIntosh, P. (1988) 'White Privilege and Male Privilege: A Personal Account of Coming to See Correspondences Through Work in Women's Studies'. Available at: https://www.racialequitytools.org/resourcefiles/mcintosh.pdf (Accessed September 7, 2023).

McIntosh, P. (2015) 'Extending the Knapsack: Using the White Privilege Analysis to Examine Conferred Advantage and Disadvantage', *Women & Therapy*, 28(3–4): 232–245.

McNeil, J., Bailey, L., Ellis, S., Morton, J., and Regan, M. (2012) 'Trans Mental Health and Emotional Wellbeing Study 2012', *Gires*. Available at: https:// www.gires.org.uk/wp-content/uploads/2014/08/trans_mh_ study.pdf (Accessed September 7, 2023).

McRuer, R. (2006) *Crip Theory: Cultural Signs of Queerness and Disability*, New York: New York University Press.

Mehra, A., Dixon, A.L. , Brass, D.J., and Robertson, B. (2006) 'The Social Network Ties of Group Leaders: Implications for Group Performance and Leader Reputation', *Organization Science*, 17(1): 64–79.

Meyer, V.F. (2001) 'The Medicalization of Menopause: Critique and Consequences', *International Journal of Health Services*, 31(4): 769–792.

Mulvey, L. (1975) 'Visual Pleasure and Narrative Cinema', *Screen*, 16(3): 6–18.

Munt, S. (1995) 'The Lesbian Flâneur', in Bell, D. and Valentine, G. (eds) *Mapping Desire: Geographies of Sexualities*, London: Routledge, pp 104–114.

Murray, S. (2008) *The 'Fat' Female Body*, Basingstoke: Palgrave Macmillan.

Naples, N.A. (2003) *Feminism and Method: Ethnography, Discourse Analysis, and Activist Research*, New York: Routledge.

Naugler, D. (2009) 'Crossing the Cosmetic/Reconstructive Divide: The Instructive Situation of Breast Reduction Surgery', in Heyes, C.J. and Jones, M.R. (eds) *Cosmetic Surgery: A Feminist Primer*, Farnham: Ashgate, pp 225–238.

NHS (nda) 'Gender Identity Services for Adults: Non-Surgical Interventions'. Available at: https://www.england.nhs.uk/wp-content/uploads/2019/07/ service- specification-gender-dysphoria-services-non-surgical-oct-2022. pdf (Accessed September 7, 2023).

NHS (ndb) 'Gender Identity Services for Adults: Surgical Interventions'. Available at: https://www.england.nhs.uk/wp-content/uploads/2019/07/ NHS- England-Service-Specification-for-Specialised-Gender-Dysphoria-Services- Surgical-v4.pdf (Accessed September 7, 2023).

NHS (2015) 'The NHS Constitution'. Available at: https://www.gov.uk/ government/ publications/the-nhs-constitution-for-england/the-nhs-constitution-for-england (Accessed September 7, 2023).

NHS (2019) 'What is Commissioning?'. Available at: https://www.england. nhs.uk/ commissioning/what-is-commissioning/ (Accessed September 8, 2023).

NHS (2023) 'Disorders of Sex Development'. Available at: https://www.nhs. uk/conditions/ disorders-sex-development/ (Accessed September 7, 2023).

Overboe, J. (2009) 'Affirming an Impersonal Life: A Different Register for Disability Studies', *Journal of Literary & Cultural Disability Studies*, 3(3): 241–256.

Palczewski, C.H., DeFrancisco, V.P., and McGeough, D.D. (2017) *Gender in Communication: A Critical Introduction*, third edn, Thousand Oaks: SAGE.

Pawluch, D. (1983) 'Transitions in Pediatrics: A Segmental Analysis', *Social Problems*, 30(4): 449–465.

Pearce, R. (2018) *Understanding Trans Health*, first edn, Bristol: Policy Press.

Phillips, C.B. (2006) 'Medicine Goes to School: Teachers as Sickness Brokers for ADHD', *PLoS Medicine*, 3(4). doi: 10.1371/journal.pmed.0030182.

Pi, S., Chou, C., and Liao, H. (2013) 'A Study of Facebook Groups Members' Knowledge Sharing', *Computers in Human Behavior*, 29(5): 1971–1979.

Ponse, B. (1976) 'Secrecy in the Lesbian World', *Journal of Contemporary Ethnography*, 5(3): 313–338.

Poster, M. (1995) 'Postmodern Virtualities', *Body & Society*, 1(3–4): 79–95.

Preciado, P.B. (2013) *Testo Junkie: Sex, Drugs, and Biopolitics in the Pharmacopornographic Era*, New York: The Feminist Press.

Raun, T. (2016) *Out Online: Trans Self-Representation and Community Building on YouTube*, Oxon: Routledge.

Rich, M. and Chalfen, R. (1999) 'Showing and Telling Asthma: Children Teaching Physicians with Visual Narrative', *Visual Sociology*, 14(1): 51–71.

Richards, C., Barker, M., Lenihan, P., and Iantaffi, A. (2014) 'Who Watches the Watchmen? A Critical Perspective on the Theorization of Trans People and Clinicians', *Feminism & Psychology*, 24(2): 248–258.

Richards, C., Arcelus, J., Barrett, J., Bouman, W.P., Lenihan, P., Lorimer, S., Murjan, S., and Seal, L. (2015) 'Trans Is Not a Disorder – But Should Still Receive Funding', *Sexual and Relationship Therapy*, 30(3): 309–313.

Rothblum, E. and Solovay, S. (eds) (2009) *The Fat Studies Reader*, New York: New York University Press.

Roughgarden, J. (2004/2013) 'Sex and Diversity, Sex Versus Gender, and Sexed Bodies; Excerpts from Evolution's Rainbow: Diversity, Gender, and Sexuality in Nature and People', in Stryker, S. and Aizura, A.Z. (eds) *The Transgender Studies Reader 2*, New York: Routledge, pp 147–155.

Royal College of Psychiatrists (2013) 'Good Practice Guidelines for the Assessment and Treatment of Adults with Gender Dysphoria'. Available at: https:// www.rcpsych.ac.uk/docs/default-source/improving-care/bet ter-mh-policy/college- reports/cr181-good-practice-guidelines-for-the- assessment-and-treatment-of- adults-with-gender-dysphoria.pdf (Accessed September 7, 2023).

Ryan, C., Huebner, D., Diaz, R.M., and Sanchez, J. (2009) 'Family Rejection as a Predictor of Negative Health Outcomes in White and Latino Lesbian, Gay, and Bisexual Young Adults', *Pediatrics*, 123(1): 346–352.

Schanzer, B., Dominguez, B., Shrout, P.E., and Caton, C.L.M. (2007) 'Homelessness, Health Status, and Health Care Use', *American Journal of Public Health*, 97(3): 464–469.

Schneider, J.W. (1978) 'Deviant Drinking as Disease: Alcoholism as a Social Accomplishment', *Social Problems*, 25(4): 361–372.

Smith, G., Bartlett, A., and King, M. (2004) 'Treatments of Homosexuality in Britain since the 1950s—An Oral History: The Experience of Patients', *The British Medical Journal*, 328. doi: 10.1136/bmj.328.427.37984.442419.EE.

Spade, D. (2000/2006) 'Mutilating Gender', in Stryker, S. and Whittle, S. (eds) *The Transgender Studies Reader*, New York: Routledge, pp 315–332.

Stoller, R.J. (1968) *Sex and Gender: The Development of Masculinity and Femininity*, London: Karnac Books.

Stone, S. (1991/2006) 'The Empire Strikes Back: A Posttranssexual Manifesto', in Stryker, S. and Whittle, S. (eds) *The Transgender Studies Reader*, New York: Routledge, pp 221–235.

Stotzer, R.L. (2009) 'Violence against Transgender People: A Review of United States Data', *Aggression and Violent Behavior*, 14(3): 170–179.

Strangio, C. (2016) 'What is a "Male Body"'. Available at: https://slate.com/human- interest/2016/07/theres-no-such-thing-as-a-male-body.html (Accessed September 7, 2023).

Stryker, S. (2006) '(De)Subjugated Knowledges: An Introduction to Transgender Studies', in Stryker, S. and Whittle, S. (eds) *The Transgender Studies Reader*, New York: Routledge, pp 1–17.

Stryker, S. and Whittle, S. (eds) (2006) *The Transgender Studies Reader*, New York: Routledge.

Talusan, M., Provenzano, B., Rodriguez, M., Solis, M., and Swartz, A. (2016) 'Unerased: Counting Transgender Lives'. Available at: https://web.archive.org/web/ 20181014101632/https://mic.com/unerased (Accessed September 7, 2023).

Tatchell, P. (2017) 'Don't Fall for the Myth that it's 50 Years Since We Decriminalised Homosexuality', *The Guardian*. Available at: https://www.theguardian.com/commentisfree/2017/ may/23/fifty-years-gay-liberation-uk-barely-four-1967-act (Accessed September 8, 2023).

Testa, R.J., Sciacca, L.M., Wang, F., Hendricks, M.L., Goldblum, P., Bradford, J., and Bognar, B. (2012) 'Effects of Violence on Transgender People', *Professional Psychology: Research and Practice*, 43(5): 452–459.

Thoren, E.M., Metze, B., Bührer, C., and Garten, L. (2013) 'Online Support for Parents of Preterm Infants: A Qualitative and Content Analysis of Facebook "Preemie" Groups', *Archives of Disease in Childhood: Fetal and Neonatal Edition*, 98(6): F538. doi: 10.1136/archdischild-2012-303572.

Thorlby, R. and Gregory, S. (2008) 'Free Choice at the Point of Referral'. Available at: https://www.kingsfund.org.uk/sites/default/files/briefing-free-choice-point-of- referral-ruth-thorlby-sarah-gregory-kings-fund-march-2008.pdf (Accessed September 8, 2023).

Tomaka, J., Thompson, S., and Palacios, R. (2006) 'The Relation of Social Isolation, Loneliness, and Social Support to Disease Outcomes Among the Elderly', *Journal of Aging and Health*, 18(3): 359–384.

Tournier, R.E. (1985) 'The Medicalization of Alcoholism: Discontinuities in Ideologies of Deviance', *Journal of Drug Issues*, 15(1): 39–49.

Trout, D.L. (1980) 'The Role of Social Isolation in Suicide', *Suicide and Life-Threatening Behavior*, 10(1): 10–23.

U.S. Department of Education Office for Civil Rights (2015) *Title IX Resource Guide*. Available at: https://www2.ed.gov/about/offices/list/ocr/docs/dcl-title-ix-coordinators-guide-201504.pdf (Accessed 7 June, 2024).

Valdes, F. (1995) 'Queers, Sissies, Dykes, and Tomboys: Deconstructing the Conflation of "Sex," "Gender," and "Sexual Orientation" in Euro-American Law and Society', *California Law Review*, 83(1): 3–10.

van Teijlingen, E.R., Lowis, G., McCaffery, P., and Porter, M. (eds) (2004) *Midwifery and the Medicalization of Childbirth: Comparative Perspectives*, New York: Nova Science Publishers.

Varela, F.J. (2001) 'Intimate Distances: Fragments for a Phenomenology of Organ Transplantation', *Journal of Consciousness Studies*, 8(5–7): 259–271.

Vincent, B. (2018) *Transgender Health: A Practitioner's Guide to Binary and Non-Binary Trans Patient Care*, London: Jessica Kingsley Publishers.

Wann, M. (2009) 'Foreword: FatStudies: An Invitation to Revolution', in Rothblum, E. and Solovay, S. (eds) *The Fat Studies Reader*, New York: New York University Press, pp ix– xxv.

West, C. and Zimmerman, D.H. (1987) 'Doing Gender', *Gender and Society*, 1(2): 125–151.

Whittle, S., Turner, L., and Al-Alami, M. (2007) *Engendered Penalties: Transgender and Transsexual People's Experiences of Inequality and Discrimination*, London: The Equalities Review.

Wood, J.M., Koch, P.B., and Mansfield, P.K. (2006) 'Women's Sexual Desire: A Feminist Critique', *The Journal of Sex Research*, 43(3): 236–244.

The World Professional Association for Transgender Health (2012) *Standards of Care for the Health of Transsexual, Transgender, and Gender Nonconforming People* [7th Version]. Available at: https://www.wpath.org/media/cms/Documents/SOC v7/SOC V7_English.pdf (Accessed September 8, 2023).

Yadegarfard, M., Meinhold-Bergmann, M.E., and Ho, R. (2014) 'Family Rejection, Social Isolation, and Loneliness as Predictors of Negative Health Outcomes (Depression, Suicidal Ideation, and Sexual Risk Behavior) Among Thai Male-to- Female Transgender Adolescents', *Journal of LGBT Youth*, 11(4): 347–363.

Zhao, S., Grasmuck, S., and Martin, J. (2008) 'Identity Construction on Facebook: Digital Empowerment in Anchored Relationships', *Computers in Human Behavior*, 24(5): 1816–1836.

Index

References to endnotes show both the page number and the note number (130n5).

A

abdominal phalloplasty 115
ableism 21
Adam, Barbara 77, 93
Adam (research participant) 3, 71
  cisnormative sex and gender attribution in healthcare 41
  Facebook 116–117
  gender archive 99
  genitals 43
  mental health 53, 83, 84–85
  misgendering, and voice 44
  self-identification 47–48
  shifting responsibility 83, 84–85
  as source of information and support 122
  trans terminology 7, 17
  wait times 89–90, 91, 104
  YouTube and vlogging 111–112
Adams, Mary Alice 7, 15
Adams, Tony 23
ADD (attention deficit disorder) 63
addiction 56, 65, 72
ADHD (attention deficit hyperactivity disorder) 63
AFAB (assigned female at birth) 8, 9, 65
ageing, medicalization of 60, 65
ageism 65
agential realism 49–50
Ahmed, S.F. 32
alcohol abuse, trans people's risk of 53
AMAB (assigned male at birth) 8, 9
American Psychiatric Association
  DSM (Diagnostic and Statistical Manual of Mental Disorders) 66
Andrews, Jorella 102, 113–114
androgen insensitivity syndrome 31
animals, hermaphrodism in 45
anti-gay laws 132n3
anti-trans architecture 98–100
anti-trans rhetoric 41
Arcelus, Jon 69–70, 82
architecture
  anti-trans 98–100
  see also space
attention deficit disorder (ADD) 63
attention deficit hyperactivity disorder (ADHD) 63
augmentation mammoplasty 13

autobiography 23
autoethnography 4, 22–23, 125–126
  autoethnography of always 24–25
  pitfalls of 130n9
  rationale for 23–24

B

Baker, Paul 133n7
Ballard, K. 66
Barad, Karen 49–50, 52
Barrett, James 69–70
barriers, to accessing healthcare 1, 2, 5–6, 41, 53, 77, 101, 102, 110, 124, 125, 127
  see also gatekeeping; medicalization
bathrooms 6, 98–100
Ben (research participant) 3, 5, 17, 56, 57, 71
  accessing healthcare 105–106
  cisnormative sex and gender attribution in healthcare 40–41
  interactional medicalization 59
  misgendering, and voice 44
  mistreatment and transphobia in healthcare 109
  negative experiences of online information-seeking 120–121
  private healthcare 79–80
  self-presentation in healthcare settings 47
  as source of information and support 123
  ticking boxes 79–80
  transmasculine identity 46–47
  wait times 93
  YouTube and vlogging 112, 114
Benjamin, Harry 106, 132n11
Bettcher, Talia Mae 28, 35, 36, 42, 47, 130n5
'beyond the binary model' 4, 34–36, 47, 54
bilateral orchidectomy 13
bilateral salpingo-oophorectomy 13
binding 51, 131n13
'biological man' 37
'biological sex' 4
'biological woman' 37
biology
  biological essentialism 41–42, 45
  disciplinary context 2
birth certificates 57
birthdays, alternative 108–109

Black people 127
Black scholars 15–16
Blackless, M. 37
Blaque, Kat 112
blogs 118
blood tests 40–41, 123
body hair removal 13
body image 51
'born male/female' terminology 7
Bornstein, Kate 2
bottom surgeries 13, 58, 80, 105
　abdominal phalloplasty 115
　bilateral orchidectomy 13
　bilateral salpingo-oophorectomy 13
　clitoroplasty 13
　glans sculpting 13
　hysterectomy 13
　metoidioplasty 13, 43, 105, 131n5
　penectomy 13
　penile prosthesis 13
　phalloplasty 13, 14, 43, 105, 122, 131n5
　scrotoplasty 13
　social media 115
　testicular prosthesis 13
　two-signature requirement for 82–83
　urethroplasty 13
　vaginectomy 13
　vaginoplasty 13
　vulvoplasty 13
　wait times 93–94
Bouman, W.P. 11, 69–70, 82, 83
Boylorn, R.M. 15, 23
Brasserie, the 98–99
breast forms 51
breast surgeries
　breast augmentation, cis women 74
　breast cancer patients 29m53, 74
　breast construction, trans women 53, 74
　breast reduction 86–87
　double mastectomy 49, 50, 75, 80, 81, 86–87, 92, 125
breasts, in sex and gender attribution 39
Brighton 98
Brown, J. 5–6, 77, 88–89
bureaucracy 5–6, 77–78, 123, 124
　axes of power 100–101, 124
　cancelled appointments 5, 78–79
　forms 5, 85–87
　institutional medicalization 57
　jumping through hoops 5, 78, 81–83
　shifting responsibility 5, 78, 83–85
　social networks 5, 87–88
　'ticking boxes' 5, 78, 79–81, 106
　weddings 122
Butler, Judith 26, 32, 36, 42

C

cancelled appointments 5, 78–79
cancer screening 104, 124, 131n3

Canguilhem, Georges 5, 67–69
Carey (research participant) 3, 55
　blogs 118
　jumping through hoops 82
　mistreatment and transphobia in healthcare 109
　as source of information and support 122
　wait times 90, 91, 92–93, 95
Case, Mary Anne C. 48–49
CCG (Clinical Commissioning Group) 13
cervical screening 10, 131n3
Chang, Heewon 15, 23
Charing Cross clinic 80, 81
Charlton, James 20
chest surgeries 13
　see also top surgery
Child and Adolescent Mental Health Services 79
childbirth, medicalization of 60, 61, 72
children
　gender policing 35
　gendered upbringing 51–52
　hyperactivity 57, 63
　medicalization 57, 63
Chrisler, J.C. 60–61
chromosomes
　attribution of sex and gender 38, 42
　intersex people 31
chronic fatigue syndrome 66
cis gaze 16
cis/cisgender terminology 7, 8
cisnormativity 2, 131n3
　sex and gender attribution in healthcare 40–41
Clinical Commissioning Group (CCG) 13
CliniQ 16
clitoris 43, 105, 131n5
clitoroplasty 13
collaboration (medical social control) 63
coming out, and Facebook 116–117
community
　loss of close ties to 10
　see also trans communities
conceptual medicalization 5, 56–57
congenital adrenal hyperplasia 31
Conrad, Peter 5, 55–56, 57, 58, 60, 61, 62, 63, 64, 65, 66, 71
conversion therapy 66–67, 71
'cosmetic' procedures 13
Cowell, Roberta 106
Crawford, Lucas 4, 6, 17–18, 77, 98–99
Creighton, Sarah 31, 32–33
CRS (critical race studies) 18, 21
CRT (critical race theory) 15–16, 18–19
cultural analysis, and personal narrative 23
cultural practices, and intersex people 32
culture, and gendering of bodies 42

D

Dan (research participant) 3
- cancelled appointments 78–79
- double mastectomy access 75, 81
- Facebook 115
- in-person support and information 121
- jumping through hoops 81–82
- mental health 83–84
- self-identification 48
- shifting responsibilities 83–84
- as source of information and support 122
- ticking boxes 79, 81
- wait times and private healthcare 13–14, 81, 91, 93–94, 104
- YouTube and vlogging 112

Davis, Lennard J. 20
deadnaming 113, 133n10
deafness 44
death, medicalization of 60
Defosse, Dana Leland 8
Delgado, Richard 15–16, 18, 19
Delph-Janiurek, Tom 51
demedicalization 1, 5, 21, 55, 65–67, 123
- challenges from physicians 69–70
- intersex people 34
- the normal and the pathological 67–69
- tension of 124–125
- unique challenges of the trans case 70–76
- see also medicalization

Department of Health 12
depathologicalization 69–70, 75–76
dermal implant 13
de-transitioning 75
deviant medicalized behavior 5
disability studies 18, 19–20, 21, 130n6
- dis/ability critical race studies (DisCrit) 21
disabled people 125
disciplinary context 1–2
discrimination, against trans people 10
doctor-patient relationships 87
- institutional medicalization 58–60
double mastectomy 49, 50, 75, 80, 81, 86–87, 92, 125
- see also breast surgery
drug abuse, trans people's risk of 53
DSM (Diagnostic and Statistical Manual of Mental Disorders), American Psychiatric Association 66
DS+R 98–99
Duguay, Stefanie 117102
Dvorsky, G. 46
dyslexia 63

E

education
- discrimination against trans people 10
- see also pedagogy; TransLiteracy

eggs
- freezing of 122
- in models of sex and gender 27–29
Elllis, Caroline 15, 22
Elston, M.A. 66
Emily (research participant) 3
- as source of information and support 122–123
- stigma 60
- ticking boxes 79
- wait times 88, 89, 94
- waiting rooms 96–97
- Yahoo 118
employment discrimination 10
- US law 48–49
English speakers 127
ethics, of trans methodology 4
ethnography 17
explicit identity statements 117

F

Facebook 6, 16, 110, 115–118
- privacy settings 134n14
facial hair removal 12
families, loss of close ties to 10
fat studies 18, 20–21, 130n6
Fausto-Sterling, Anne 4, 27
female bodies 4, 28, 42
- voices 44
'female' bodily components 38
female-bodied 3738
feminine, terminology 8–9
feminism
- medicalization of natural life processes 60–61
Feminist Standpoint Theory 129n5
feminist studies, disciplinary context 2
Flora (research participant) 3, 4, 17
- cancelled appointments 79
- in-person support and information 121–122
- private healthcare 91–92, 97–98
- as source of information and support 122
- Twitter 119, 120
- waiting rooms 97–98
forms, structure of 5, 85–87
Foucault, Michel 64
France, medical bureaucracy 80
free choice principle, NHS 11
friends, loss of close ties to 10

G

Garfinkel, Harold 9
gatekeeping 5–6, 57, 63, 72, 124, 125
- see also bureaucracy
gender 4–5
- cultural construction of 26
- gendered upbringing 51–52
- in healthcare 37

intra-acting gender 49–52
models of 4, 26
  beyond the binary 34–36, 47, 54
  challenging the narrative 29–36
  egg and sperm 27–29
  intersex people 31–34
  reintegration with sex 48–54
  self-identification of 49
  sex and gender attribution 37–40
    biological essentialism 41–42, 45
    in healthcare 40–41
and sociology 2
gender archive 99, 100
gender discrimination, US law 48–49
gender dysphoria diagnosis 5, 29, 56, 57, 71–72, 73, 76
'gender dysphoria pathway,' NHS
  adult non-surgical services 12
  adult surgical services 12–13
  youth service 12
gender euphoria 116, 134n16
gender expression 9, 46
  sexual intermediaries 31
gender identity
  explicit identity statements 117
  intersex people 32
  sexual intermediaries 30, 31
gender Identity clinics (GICs) *see* GICs (gender Identity clinics)
gender identity disorder diagnosis 5, 55
gender markers 58, 103, 124, 134n1
'gender outlaws' 2
gender policing, of children 35
gender presentation, knowledge about 103
Gender Recognition Certificates (GRCs) 57, 100, 103
gender stereotypes 27
General Practitioners (GPs) *see* GPs (General Practitioners)
genital appearance
  attribution of sex and gender 38–39, 42–43
  intersex people 31–34
  and sex assigned at birth 7
genitalia, sexual intermediaries 30
George (research participant) 3, 75
  bathrooms 99
  and bureaucracy 77
  jumping through hoops 82
  as source of information and support 122
Gergen, K.J. 15, 24
Gergen, M.M. 15, 24
GICs (gender Identity clinics) 12–13
  knowledge about 103–104
  non-surgical adult services 12
  Nottingham GIC 69, 82
  referrals to 6, 11–12, 58–60, 73, 121, 122
  remit of in the NHS 12–13

  self-referral 85–86, 132n6
  Tavistock and Portman GIC 69
  wait times 11, 89–90
glans sculpting 13
GoFundMe 74
Gorman, J.A. 60–61
GPs (General Practitioners) 11–12, 121
  institutional medicalization 58–60
  knowledge about 103, 106
GRCs (Gender Recognition Certificates) 57, 100, 103
Grosz, Elizabeth 42, 51

H

hair transplantation 13
harassment 111, 113
Harris, Angela 19
hatred, of the body 34
health, scope of 9–10
healthcare
  as a bureaucracy 5–6
  cisnormative sex and gender attribution in 40–41
  mistreatment and transphobia in 109–110
  negative experiences of 109–110, 119, 133n1
  trans healthcare system 124, 127–128
  trans people's self-presentation in 46, 47
  see also GICs (gender Identity clinics); GPs (General Practitioners); mental health services; NHS (National Health Service); private healthcare
hermaphrodism, in animals and plants 45
hermaphrodites 30
  see also sexual intermediaries
Hirschfeld, Magnus 29–31
HIV/AIDS 70
Holly (research participant) 3, 127
  Instagram 118–119
  as source of information and support 123
  Twitter 120
  YouTube and vlogging 112
homosexuality
  demedicalization of 5, 66, 67, 68, 76, 125
  medicalization of 62, 70–71, 72
hormones
  intersex people 31
  see also HRT (hormone replacement therapy)
housing, discrimination against trans people 10
HRT (hormone replacement therapy) 5, 29, 56, 71, 72–73, 80
  intersex people 33
  knowledge about 103
  medical transition 9, 10
  NHS services 12, 14
  wait times 92

Hughes, I.A. 32, 33
Hughes, James 46, 52–53
human fertilization, gendered metaphors in 27–28
human rights, intersex people 33
hysterectomy 13

I

ideology (medical social control) 63
indigenous scholars 15–16
informed consent 33, 70, 71, 74, 75, 76, 124, 125, 126
Ingrid (research participant) 3, 109
 as source of information and support 122
 Twitter 119–120
in-person support and information 121–123
insider research 24
Instagram 6, 118–119
institutional medicalization 5, 56, 57
interactional medicalization 5, 56, 58–60
International Classification of Diseases, WHO 66
internet, the 6, 110
 as form of decentralized communication 110–111
 restricted access to 133n12
 see also social media
intersectionality 19
intersex people 8, 9, 31–34, 37, 42, 49, 52, 130n6
 presenting as, to access transition-related healthcare 106
interview style 16–17, 125
intra-action 49–52, 105
Israeli-Nevo, Atalia 77, 95–96, 102, 104

J

Jackson, Stevi 51–52
Johnson, J.L. 29, 46, 47
Jones, Stacy Holman 15, 23
jumping through hoops 5, 78, 81–83

K

Kessler, Suzanne 38–40
Klinefelter syndrome 31

L

language 7–9
 Polari 133n7
 trans dialect 108–109
 trans terminology 6–7
 see also conceptual medicalization
Latham, J.R. 4, 25, 34, 102, 105, 129n1, 133n5
Lenihen, Penny 69–70
lesbians, covert identification of each other 107–108

LGBTQ people
 anti-gay laws 132n3
 disclosure of on social media 117
 Polari 133n7
Liao, L. 33
lipoplasty/contouring 13
liver transplant surgery 5–6, 87, 88–89
London, bias towards in research 127
Lorimer, Stuart 10, 69–70

M

Maister, David H. 77, 94–95
male bodies 4, 42
 voices 44
'male' bodily components 38
'male gaze' 129n3
male-bodied 28, 37, 38
Martin, Emily 4, 27, 41
masculine, terminology 8–9
masculinizing chest liposuction 13
mastectomy, double 13, 49, 50, 58, 75, 80, 81, 86–87, 92, 125
 see also breast surgery
McKenna, Wendy 38–40
medical anthropology, disciplinary context 1–2
'medical gaze' 64–65
medical professionals
 interactional medicalization 58–60
 lack of training/understanding of trans patients 41, 53
 nature of, and medicalization 63–64
medical social control 5, 56, 57, 64–65
medicalization 5, 29, 55–56, 65–66, 124, 130n2
 challenges from physicians 69–70
 conceptual 5, 56–57
 deviant and natural life course medicalized behavior 5, 56, 60–62
 of human body diversity 21
 institutional 5, 56, 57
 interactional 5, 56, 58–60
 medical social control 5, 56, 57, 64–65
 nature of the medical profession 63–64
 the normal and the pathological 67–69
 and secularization 62–63
 see also demedicalization
medicalized social control 5
medicine, disciplinary context 2
menopause, medicalization of 60, 61
menstruation, medicalization of 60, 61, 62
mental health, and wait times 89
mental health services
 forms 86
 knowledge about 104
 misgendering, and voice 44
 trans people's difficulty in accessing 53
methodology see trans methodology
metoidioplasty 13, 43, 105, 131n5

Index

microdermabrasion 13
misgendering 17, 44, 113
'morphological self-determination' 52–53
Mulvey, Laura 129n3
Munt, Sally 77
murder, trans people's risk of 10
Murjan, Sarah 69–70
Mx. title 134n1

N

name changing 9, 58, 103, 116, 117, 124
'natal gender' terminology 7
National Transgender Discrimination Survey 131n15
natural life course medicalized behavior 5
Naugler, Diane 77, 86, 87
negative experiences of healthcare 109–110, 119, 133n1
NHS (National Health Service) 10–12, 66
  Constitution 11
  'gender dysphoria pathway' 12–13
  'gender dysphoria'/'gender identity disorder' diagnosis 5, 55
  hospital ward accommodation 11, 124
  intersex people 33
  NHS Mandate (England) 12
  Patient Choice Scheme 11–12
  patients' rights 11
  policies, knowledge about 104
  wait times policy 11, 13–14, 89, 90
  see also bureaucracy
nipple grafting 13
nipple repositioning 13
nipple tattooing 13
nipple-areolar complex modification 13
non-binary people 73–74, 100, 130n5, 5254
  beyond the binary model of sex and gender 34, 36
  bodies 42
  exclusion from legal recognition 57
  self-presentation in healthcare settings 47
  terminology 8, 9, 22
non-human bodies 50
non-transition-related healthcare 1, 9, 104
normal, the 67–69
normalcy 20
Northampton clinic 80, 81
Nottingham 98
Nottingham GIC 69, 82

O

objectivity 21
ODD (oppositional defiant disorder) 63
offline education 121–123
older people 127
Open Barbers 16
Orbe, M.P. 15, 23
orchidectomy 13
"Other" 23

P

packers 51, 105, 131n10
Palczewski, C.H. 129n2
pap smears 10, 131n3
passing 9, 44, 75
pathological, the 67–69
Pawluch, Dorothy 63–64
Pearce, Ruth 9, 24, 73, 75–76, 77, 88, 102, 109, 110, 119, 133n1
pedagogy 6, 102–104, 123, 126–127
  finding of trans communities 107–108
  negative experiences of healthcare 109–110, 119, 133n1
  offline education 121–123
  personal narrative 6, 23, 102, 104–107
  social media 6, 16, 110–121
pediatrics, expansion of 63–64
penectomy 13
penile prosthesis 13
penis
  different types of 51
  genital appearance 43
  personal narrative 105
  sex and gender attribution 39
  see also bottom surgeries
people of color 15–16, 18–19, 21, 125, 127
performativity 50
personal narrative 6, 23, 102, 104–107
phalloplasty 13, 14, 43, 105, 122, 131n5
philosophy, disciplinary context 2
phonosurgery 13
physical assault, trans people's risk of 10, 53
plants, hermaphrodism in 45
PMDD (premenstrual dysphoric disorder) 61
PMS (premenstrual syndrome), medicalization of 60, 61
Polari 133n7
Ponse, Barbara 102, 107–108
Poster, Mark 6, 102, 110–111, 113
postgenderism 45–48, 54
post-traumatic stress disorder, intersex people 33
power 5–6
  axes of 100–101, 124
Preciado, Paul B. 4, 17, 35, 42, 44, 77, 80
pregnancy, medicalization of 60, 61, 62
premenstrual dysphoric disorder (PMDD) 61
premenstrual syndrome (PMS), medicalization of 60, 61
private healthcare 11, 13–14, 79–80, 81, 88, 97–98
  knowledge about 103–104
  wait times 13–14, 88, 91–92, 93

privilege 15, 87, 129n2
pronouns 117, 124
　gender-neutral 3, 17, 46
　pronoun badges 108
　research participants' choice of 3
　social transition 9, 59
prostate exams 10
psychology, disciplinary context 2
psychotherapy 5, 10, 79
public funding, of healthcare in the UK 11
　see also NHS (National Health Service)
public health factors 10

Q

queer studies, disciplinary context 2

R

race, as a social construct 19
racism 19, 21
　see also CRT (critical race theory)
Raun, Tobias 102, 113
real life experience (RLE) 58, 73
　see also social transition
refugees 125
religion
　secularization and medicalization 62–63
repetitive strain injury 66
reproductive organs
　intersex people 31–34
　sexual intermediaries 30
Repta, R. 29, 46, 47
research
　importance of 2
　limitations of 127
　outline of 2–4
　see also trans methodology
responsibility, shifting of 5, 78, 83–85
rhinoplasty 13
Richards, Christina 69–70, 82, 83
Rokitansky syndrome 31
Rothblum, E. 20
Roughgarden, Joan 41, 45
Royal College of Psychiatrists 95

S

scholars of color 15–16
schools
　institutional medicalization 57
　see also children; education
Scott, Sue 51–52
scrotoplasty 13
Seal, Leighton 69–70
secondary sexual characteristics
　sex and gender attribution 43–44
　sexual intermediaries 30
secularization, and medicalization 62–63
self-referral forms 85–86, 125
sex 4–5, 126
　attribution 37–40, 42–45, 51

biological essentialism 41–42, 45
　in healthcare 37, 40–41
models of 4, 26
　beyond the binary 34–36, 47, 54
　challenging the narrative 29–36
　egg and sperm 27–29
　intersex people 31–34
　sexual intermediaries 29–31
　reintegration of 48–54
　self-identification of 35–36, 49, 52–54
　social construction of 37
sex assigned at birth 8
　and genital appearance 7
sex binary 35, 37, 45
　and intersex people 31
"sex change" 42
'sex of rearing,' intersex people 32
sexism 65
sexual assault, trans people's risk of 10
sexual discrimination, US law 48–49
sexual intermediaries 29–31
sexuality, medicalization of 60
shifting responsibility 5, 78, 83–85
sign language 44
Smith, G. 62
social control see medicalized social control
social internet 103
　as form of decentralized
　　communication 110–111
　see also social media
social isolation
　misgendering, and voice 44
social media 110–121
　Facebook 6, 16, 110, 115–118
　Instagram 6, 118–119
　and pedagogy 6
　Twitter 6, 117, 119
　Yahoo 118
　YouTube and vlogging 6, 110, 111–115
social networks 5, 87–88
social transition 5, 12, 58, 73, 103
social welfare services, UK 72
sociology, disciplinary context 2
Solovay, S. 20
space 6, 77, 100, 123, 124
　anti-trans architecture 98–100
　hospital ward accommodation 11, 124
　waiting rooms 96–98
Spade, Dean 4, 24–25, 46, 102, 106, 107
sperm, in models of sex and gender 27–29
Stefancic, J. 18, 19
stigma 5, 55, 59–60, 61, 65, 66, 69,
　75, 124
Stoller, Robert J. 130n1
Stone, S. 106
Strangio, Chase 54
strap-ons 51, 105, 131n11
Stryker, Susan 1, 24–25
suicide, trans people's risk of 10, 53, 62

Index

surgical procedures 5, 29, 56, 57, 71–72, 72–73
  intersex infants 31, 32–33
  knowledge about 103
  medical transition 9, 10
  NHS 12–13
  see also bottom surgeries; top surgeries
surveillance (medical social control) 63

T

talking therapies, NHS services 12
Tavistock and Portman GIC 69
'T-day' 108–109
technology (medical social control) 63
telephones, as decentralized communication 110, 111
terminology 7–9
  trans terminology 6–7
  umbrella terms 22
testicular prosthesis 13
testosterone 35, 120
  cisnormative sex and gender attribution in healthcare 40–41
  gel 93, 122
  low dose 122
  'T-day' 108–109
thyroid chondroplasty 13
'ticking boxes' 5, 78, 79–81, 106
time 5–6, 77, 104, 123
  wait times 5–6, 11, 13–14, 88–96, 100, 124, 125
Title IX, US law 48, 131n9
toilet facilities 6, 98–100
top surgeries 13
  augmentation mammoplasty 13
  breast construction, trans women 53, 74
  double mastectomy 49, 50, 75, 80, 81, 86–87, 92, 125
  masculinizing chest liposuction 13
  nipples 13
  self-assessment 125
trans communities 2
  finding of 107–108
  research and information accessibility 17–18, 126
trans dialect 6, 108–109
trans flag 108
trans men, intra-acting gender 50–51
Trans Mental Health Study 131n15
trans methodology 1, 4, 15–18, 123, 125–126
  autoethnography 22–25
  CRT (critical race theory) 15–16, 18–19
  differentiation of 21–22
  disability studies 18, 19–20, 21
  fat studies 18, 20–21
  interview style 16–17
  limitations of 22

trans people
  covert identification of each other 108
  and the gendering of body parts 28
  institutional medicalization 57
  and postgenderism 45–48, 54
  self-presentation in healthcare settings 46, 47
  sex and gender attribution 39
  stereotypes of 73
  suicide risk 10, 53, 62
  'wrong body' model 4, 28, 29, 34, 35, 36, 54, 73, 130n5
trans studies 1, 2, 15, 16, 21, 25
trans★ terminology 18
trans women 127
#transdocfail 119
transexual terminology 129n1
transfeminine 28, 127
  terminology 8, 9
transgender architecture 6
transgender studies *see* trans studies
transgender terminology 7
transitioning
  funding of 74
  medical transition 9
  and sex self-identification 52
  social transition 9, 12, 58, 73, 103
  taking time with 95–96
  terminology 9
transition-related healthcare 1, 9, 10, 124
  demedicalization 124–125
  knowledge about 103
  personal narrative around accessing of 105–107
  self-assessment 125
TransLiteracy 6, 102, 103–104, 123, 126–127
  finding of trans communities 107–108
  negative experiences of healthcare 109–110, 119, 133n1
  offline education 121–123
  personal narrative 6, 23, 102, 104–107
  social media 6, 16, 110–121
transmasculine 28, 34
  terminology 8, 9
transness
  conceptual medicalization 56–57
  as 'deviant' behavior 60, 61–62
  not a disorder 124
  stigmatization of 5, 59, 60
transphobia 2, 115
  in healthcare 109–110
tuberculosis 66
tucking 51, 105, 131n12
Turner syndrome 31
Twitter 6, 117, 119

U

umbrella terms 22
  see also terminology

universities 122
   challenge to role of 18
urethroplasty 13
US law 48–49

V

vaginectomy 13
vaginoplasty 13
Varela, Francisco J. 77, 87
Vincent, Ben 37, 58–59, 77, 84, 132n15
vlogging 6, 110, 111–115
voice, the
   sex and gender attribution 44–45
   voice and communication
      therapies 12, 44
'voice-of-color thesis' 19
'voice-of-trans thesis' 19
vulva, sex and gender attribution 39
vulvoplasty 13

W

wait times 5–6, 11, 88–90, 100
   factors making wait easier 94–95
   knowledge about 104
   private healthcare 13–14, 88, 91–92, 93
   taking time 95–96
   unclear 90–94
waiting rooms 6, 96–98
Wales 109
Wann, Marilyn 20, 21
wedding bureaucracies 122
white supremacy 19
Whittle, Stephen 24–25
World Health Organization (WHO) 66
World Professional Association for
   Transgender Health, The 10
'worst-case scenarios' 109–110
writing style 17, 126
   see also language
'wrong body' model 4, 28, 29, 34, 35, 36, 54, 73, 130n5

Y

Yahoo 118
young people 127
   'gender dysphoria pathway,' NHS 12
YouTube 6, 110, 111–115

Z

Zhao, S. 102, 117

www.ingramcontent.com/pod-product-compliance
Lightning Source LLC
Chambersburg PA
CBHW071712020426
42333CB00017B/2239